THE CONSECRATED LIFE

THE CONSECRATED LIFE

Crossroads and Directions

Marcello Azevedo, S.J.

Translated by
Guillermo Cook

ORBIS BOOKS

Maryknoll, New York 10545

The Catholic Foreign Mission Society of America (Maryknoll) recruits and trains people for overseas missionary service. Through Orbis Books, Maryknoll aims to foster the international dialogue that is essential to mission. The books published, however, reflect the opinions of their authors and are not meant to represent the official position of the society.

ORBIS/ISBN 1-57075-003-3   GRACEWING/ISBN 0-85244-337-4

In gratitude to the Lord of my life, I also thankfully dedicate this book to all the people who, throughout all of my fifty years of consecration for mission in the Society of Jesus, helped me to rediscover my Bearings in the Crossroads of Life.

Contents

Part 3

MISSION AND CONSECRATION
Spirituality and Prospects

A Note on Terminology

Following a popular and nontechnical set of meanings, as well as canonically defined usages, this book uses a body of terminology centering on what Catholics call consecrated life, consecrated religious life, and religious life.

The terms *religious life* and/or *consecrated religious life* refer to the way of life and/or to the institution of living a common life by members of a given community (also called a congregation, an order, or a religious institute) under the vows of poverty, obedience, and chastity (celibacy), and sometimes other vows, according to the rules and constitutions of institutes approved by the hierarchy of the Roman Catholic Church.

As popularly used, *religious life* and *consecrated religious life* are a general way of referring to the ensemble of diverse institutes that, taken as a whole and considered as a distinct vocation in the church, are in contrast to presbyterial, diaconal, episcopal, and lay vocations.

The noun *religious* will be used in this book to designate the members (male or female) who live the consecrated religious life. The expression *religious vocations*—in the plural—draws attention to the fact that the religious vocation as such has taken different forms in the course of history (for example, the monastic and mendicant models).

The term *consecrated life* has a broader meaning. It includes the first meaning of consecrated religious life as defined above. Second, it encompasses the so-called secular institutes, wherein lay persons (both men and women) live their lives as single or married persons who live professional lives in the secular world. Such secular institutes also may include priests who are consecrated in a special way by particular vows, promises, or commitments.

In order to be complete, though at the risk of becoming less precise, we must also mention members of groups called Societies of Apostolic Life. These are associations of men or women who band together for certain apostolic purposes. The Roman congregation formerly known as the Sacred Congregation for Religious Life and Secular Institutes, which is in charge of religious life, recently changed its name. It is now called the Congregation for the Institutes of Consecrated Life and Societies of Apostolic Life to reflect this broad category of dedicated persons.

Prologue

This book does not offer a theoretical discussion of the religious life. Nor is it a collection of biblical texts, or a compilation of documentary sources. I could have chosen any of these options.

Sacred Scripture—with its inexhaustible riches—is available to us. It can be read, as it usually is, from well-defined and diverse perspectives. Even though I am not concerned about citing scripture as a proof text, this work has a solid biblical foundation.

There is also an abundance of documents about the religious vocations. The conciliar magisterium highlighted the religious life with the constitution *Lumen Gentium* and the decree *Perfectae Caritatis.* The post-conciliar magisterium gave ample attention to the ecclesial vocation of religious consecration. To mention only a few of the most important and far-reaching documents, let us remember the decisive Motu Proprio *Ecclesiae Sanctae* (1966), the Instruction *Renovationis Causam* (1969), the Apostolic Exhortation *Evangelica Testificatio* (1971), the Instruction *Mutuae Relationes* (1978), and the Apostolic Exhortation *Redemptionis Donum* (1984). Also worthy of note are the statements of the Sacred Congregation of Religious and Secular Institutes entitled "Religious and Human Promotion" and "The Contemplative Dimension of the Religious Life" (1980), not to mention, of course, the new Code of Canon Law (1983) and the various letters of John Paul II. These and other texts are aimed at every aspect of religious life, viewed from a universal perspective. One might add to this list the part played by the discourses of John Paul II in the chapters of various institutes, or speaking to male and female religious in the various countries that he visited.

Beyond these documents of the universal church, there has been no lack of valuable commentary in the great documents that have been produced by continental episcopal conferences and assemblies, such as Medellín, Puebla, and Santo Domingo—to cite examples only from Latin America. Also, meetings of the superiors general of religious orders and national conferences—and regional and continental confederations—of religious have multiplied their reflections and publications in the context of well-defined and very challenging local situations. However, aware as I am of the impressive array of biblical texts and ecclesiastical documents on the subject of the religious vocation, I shall not refer to them. I want to avoid a textual "collage," which might easily double the length of this book.

I do, however, wish to share my own vision on several key issues, responding to particular problems and to current and specific challenges. I should like to help not so much by repeating what has already been said and decreed but by reflecting upon matters that need to be deepened, affirmed, debated, or resolved. The tenor of this book is one of concerned realism and open-ended searching.

The Preparation of This Book

This work has been a long time in the making. Its preparation followed two parallel routes. On the one hand there is the experience of a lifetime. What I am sharing here has been absorbed mostly in prayer. I came to reflect more on this subject particularly during my jubilee year. With great gratitude to the Lord and to so many people, I reached my fiftieth year of service as a religious on February 2, 1994. This book is a kind of milestone to mark this date. The lives of so many people and groups, congregations, and institutes with whom I was privileged to work—especially during the past twenty years—have also contributed to the making of this book. During this time I was involved in a variety of ministries: individual counselling, spiritual direction and advising, teaching courses and seminars, leading study sessions, doing retreats, participating in assemblies and chapters of religious, and many other ways of presence and action.

In the past six years I have had the opportunity to speak in Rome to more than 2,000 superiors general of male and female orders in five different assemblies. I have spoken in Brazil to more than 3,000 religious, both men and women, in different centers. In Italy I spoke to 640 provincials and generals; in France to 720; and in English and French Canada, to 650; in Belgium to 1,100 French-speaking mothers superior and trainers; in the Caribbean to 115 major superiors of the congregations that operate in the region. Although the latter have a common Creole cultural background, they are diversified by Spanish, French, English, and Dutch colonial roots. In Haiti I addressed some 800 of the religious, all of the bishops and the majority of the clergy in that troubled country. Along with these localized corporative opportunities, I was invited to speak at the general or provincial level in numerous institutes, chapters, and assemblies, and taught courses to national and international audiences.

These events were preceded by long periods of specific preparation, with extensive reading of background material that was made available to me, interviews, and the like. For several of these occasions I was asked to prepare materials which were later published. The direct contact with so many people and diverse realities, in spite of the uniformity of the religious life, became the stuff of my reflection.

My reflection is, however, incomplete. Above all, I am lacking the personal experience and firsthand knowledge of the religious vocations in Africa and Asia. I am convinced more and more that these continents will be a rich source of cultural and spiritual inspiration for the renewal of religious life.

Background and Research

Alongside my personal experiences and the opportunities to write on the subject, I have been able to research extensively on the topic of the religious life. I have studied a variety of works in several languages on the theme of the vocational identity and its application to apostolic and pastoral mission. The results of my research have been published in books and dictionaries, and in Latin American, European, and North American journals on the religious life. My interaction with students on my books has been particularly helpful.

Despite the abundance of material that this research has made available to me, I have chosen not to write a narrative work, full of case studies and examples. I have also tried to avoid making this a scholarly work with the requisite footnoting.

My principal focus is Latin America, and in particular Brazil. It is from here that I view and understand the world. I am reflecting in the context of a continent and nation where religious life has been creative. They have demonstrated sensitivity to the reality in which they live and a capacity of coping with the challenges that are thrown at them by an environment which is difficult, contradictory, and confusing. I do not, however, give pride of place to the religious experience in Latin America and Brazil, as if this were somehow qualitatively superior. A long and varied international experience has shown me that, in our day and time, models and institutions, initiatives and information spread rapidly and interact through channels of communication. Many elements that people commonly consider to be characteristic of the religious life in this or that region of the world—such as insertion in Latin America, or inculturation in Africa and Asia—can be found elsewhere. While the colors and styles may be unique, one can always find a similarity of outlooks and a commonality of interpretations.

What I expound and share in this book seems to me present today in the question of religious vocations throughout the world, with greater or lesser emphasis in given local circumstances. It is because of this that I suspect that this work may be of greater value to international congregations, but I hope it will be useful to local congregations as well.

I have labored to present a work unencumbered by intellectual pretensions. I hope, however, that it does not lack the wisdom that was imparted to me by so many people through numerous experiences and in specific contexts. This is a thematic work, yet not exhaustive. It lays out in an orderly fashion some of the great matters that have been faced during the post-conciliar period by a religious life that is consecrated and actively apostolic within the Catholic church, especially in the West.

The adjectives *apostolic* and *active* that I use to qualify the religious life are frequently used in writing on this topic. Yet they are not fully adequate, because they are applied usually to "active religious." Still, strictly speaking, the terms are not exclusive to this form of the consecrated life. The contemplative life is also apostolic and active, although in its own way. These caveats notwithstanding, I shall bow to common usage.

This book, therefore, deals with the active religious life. This coincides at many points with the contemplative life, but the latter is not the subject of this work. When I have occasion to refer to the monastic life, I have in mind above all contemplative monasticism, even though I am aware that there are many monastic structures that are living an active and non-cloistered religious life.

I am guided also by an observation which comes from both historical and theological experience. Over the centuries there have been great transformations and sharp breaks in the consecrated way of life that have altered models and reshaped forms. However, the one constant (with rare exceptions, such as in the military orders) is not the substitution pure and simple of one model for another, due to the demise of the original paradigms, but continuity in the midst of discontinuity. Unique institutions have succumbed. But, what does remain, albeit with profound modifications, are the spiritual traditions and their foundational institutions which are rooted in the gospel.

All this information and clarification is important so that one does not expect from this book what it cannot or must not deliver. I am dealing here with a modest project, which I do not pretend covers every situation. I shall be silent about many burning questions—such as the mutual relationships among bishops and religious, the matter of community, and of vows. I have dealt with these topics in other of my works.

This work is divided into three parts. The first consists of five chapters and deals with the interrelationship among vocation, mission, evangelization, apostolate, and the pastoral ministry. The qualifications for all these, as they pertain to the religious life, are examined through the lens of inculturation, which relates culture to both faith and charism. I conclude with an option which is evangelical and ecclesial, prophetic and solidary—giving preference for "the poor." This is the liberating axis of a religious life which is both present and future in orientation.

The second part deals with religious life in its formal sense and the dynamics of its transformation in the difficult context of the structures of community in the First and Third Worlds (Latin America in particular). Although they are imprecise and incomplete, the categories of "First" and "Third" worlds can still be used here, with the limitations that I shall place upon them.

The third part of this work asks questions regarding a spirituality that is fundamentally evangelical. Hopefully, it underlies the diverse charisms that various traditions have structured and consolidated over time. The last chapter attempts to bring together a possible profile for the future of religious life in the West.

Materials in some chapters have been presented in courses, papers, articles, and publications, but have been edited and reworked for this book. This means that certain subjects will reappear under different rubrics in a way that I hope addresses a variety of concerns. I have chosen to maintain thematic unity, while occasionally exploring particular subjects in depth at risk of repetition. The repetitions, some of which are intentional, emphasize the importance of particular topics for the author. They also illustrate the versatile and complex character of the questions at hand.

I wish to express my deep thankfulness to the Lord for having allowed me to live during the past fifty years as a religious. I have tried to express what I have come to understand about religious life in a time of "transformations." I have been witness to many of these transformations and an actor and initiator on a few occasions. I have experienced meaningfulness in the process and possibilities for helping build the Kingdom in service to God and to God's people in this very concrete world of ours.

I wish also to express thanks to all those people who shared in my life and who have had an influence upon it. As I express my gratitude to them, I ask them to join me in thanking the Lord of our lives.

THE CONSECRATED LIFE

Part 1

VOCATION AND CONSECRATION
FOR MISSION

1

Vocation

Biblical Foundation and Dynamic

The Semantics of Vocation

Vocation is a theme that is central to the Christian life in general, and particularly to the consecrated life. We usually think of the Christian life in terms of our individual presence and action in the world, as persons and families who live and work day by day in faith, hope, and love. There is much truth in this. But we should also see vocation as a dynamic interaction that takes place within ourselves, between God and ourselves, and between ourselves and the world. Through these interactions we are called to bring about the Kingdom of God. We are not, therefore, isolated beings, but part of a people that has been called by God to live and promote life. This purpose of vocation—the foundation and guiding star of Christian life—is expressed succinctly by Jesus when he says: "I have come that they may have life and have it to the full" (Jn 10:10).

For several centuries the word *vocation* has been tied semantically to a clerical, episcopal, or presbyterial monopoly. To promote or to pray for vocations was the same as to search for new candidates for the priesthood or to support and train them. Only recently have we Catholics retrieved the biblical teaching that every Christian has an active mission in the world and is especially called to this by God. Each one of us has a vocation to fulfill.

Vocation signifies a specific call from the Lord. From a theological and sacramental perspective, our vocation is specifically enunciated very early in life, in baptism and later in confirmation. From our youth onward, our vocation becomes clearer and more explicit, freer and more responsible. In sum, our call or vocation is oriented toward mission—

3

toward a particular way of being and acting—that should encompass and pervade every aspect of our being.

Mission must not be confused with function. The latter has a pragmatic, and above all an active character. It is usually temporary and has a less deep relationship to a person's being. Persons can exercise different functions simultaneously, and can move from one to another without implying any profound change in their life orientations or worldview. Mission, therefore, is not what we do. What we can do and really should be is an expression of mission, but should not be confused or identified with function.

Keeping this distinction between function and mission in mind, we can understand that there is a multiplicity of functions and missions. At the same time, considering the diversity of missions and their relationship to vocation, we can speak with greater precision about vocations in the plural. In fact, there is a multitude of vocations, calls that we receive from God and that are manifested in each one of us. In principle, we can say that every person has a mission to perform in this world and in history. Each one of us is a specific and unrepeatable expression of the love of God. This individuality is what identifies us. It expresses the unique character of our real or potential contribution to humanity. It is as unmistakable as the timbre of our voices, handwriting, fingerprints, genes, and DNA. It is as unique as our temperaments and personalities, the specificity of our vocations. The God who calls us unto life, in the midst of our daily lives, calls us to become present in the world in ways unique to each one of us. Human history is a complex tapestry in which are worked, over time, the strands of our unique personal histories, histories woven from the threads of our being a people, our common and diverse cultures, blood lines, family relationships, and shared traditions.

Vocation, Communion, and Communication

The call to mission is one of the evidences of the love of God, who communicates with us God's own unique creation. God inspires us, challenges us, and points the way forward; God guides, directs, strengthens, and thrusts us forward, again and again. We can say, then, that vocation is one of the expressions of the Word of God—of this God who, because God is love, is consequently also word and communication. There is, though, such a thing as one-way communication. The newscast every evening, for example, gives us one-way communication, information about world events. We receive it and store it for future reference.

But full communication does not take place if there is no response to the word that has been sent forth. Such communication takes place only between one who speaks and one who responds. The vocation that I have in mind is a process of full communication. God speaks and we respond. It is therefore fundamental to identify the language and the message of God in order for us to respond to the Lord.

Although each of us has a personal vocation, we also know that there are groups that have a vocational affinity. Several persons may be called to serve in common or analogous ways. The thousands of people in a large airport terminal may be intent upon traveling on a particular day to fulfill their own interests and responsibilities. Yet, each one has a particular goal and destination. When a certain flight is called, an ad hoc group gathers in the same departure lounge. They are separated from the mass of people who are traveling on the same day—an identifiable group of passengers that will travel on the same flight. Similarly, we are all called to live as human beings. But we belong to a variety of cultures, to this or that nationality, family, or profession. We live our particular histories in the midst of a shared human history. All these factors progressively define us, so that in the midst of diversity we discover our affinity with other people.

Christian Vocations

The Christian faith, lived out conscientiously in history, has developed and shaped many of the Christian vocations to which we dedicate ourselves today. I use, of course, a particular Roman Catholic vocabulary in talking this way. Among the people of God we have the diaconal, presbyterial, and episcopal vocations in pastoral ministry. There is the consecrated religious vocation, whether priestly or otherwise. We have the lay vocation, which may or may not be consecrated. These three broad classes group and define fundamentally Christian vocation in the Roman Catholic communion today: the clergy (juridically limited to males only), religious (male and female), and laity (male and female).

Within each of these fundamental vocational groups, there are innumerable possible variations. Returning to the image of the airport, passengers flying to the same destination may travel on different airlines. This means that they must be grouped according to several categories of time-slots, departure lounges, and types of on-board services. They also have the possibility of connecting flights. Similarly, in the Catholic church there is one episcopal order but many bishops, and great variations in dioceses. A large number of persons bear the common name "religious," but they belong to different religious traditions (Benedictines, Augustinians, Jesuits, Franciscans, Dominicans, Carmelites, and so forth). Each tradition includes different kinds of congregations and institutes—for example, within the male Franciscans, there are Friars Minor, Capuchins, Conventuals, and Third Order Friars.

None of this is of recent vintage, nor is it merely accidental. Human beings have a deep need to express their diversity, and this includes diverse expressions of the divine invitation that we call a vocation. The Bible illustrates this in the life of Israel, a people that is so significant to our faith. Scripture is full of stories about vocations in which men and women today, in all walks of life, can find themselves and see themselves reflected. Let us consider a few of these cases, after which we shall reflect upon the meaning of vocation based upon the combined texts.

Biblical Stories about Vocations

Old Testament vocational stories include the following . . . foundational: Abraham (Gn 12:1-3) and Moses (Ex 3); judges (Jgs 6:11-23); royal (1 Sm 10:17-27; 16:1-12); prophetic (Is 6:1-13; 40:1-11; Jer 1:4-10; Ez 1-3; Am 7:14-15); the Servant of Yahweh (Is 42:1-17); the pagans (1 Kgs 19:15; Is 44:28; 45:1-5; 46:11; 48:14-15); the vocation of parenthood (Gn 18:1-15—Sarah; 5:22,23—Rebecca; Jgs 13—Samson's mother).

New Testament vocational stories include the following . . . Zechariah and Elizabeth (Lk 1:5-25); Mary (Lk 1:30-35—messianic parenthood); Joseph (Mt 1:20,21—adoptive parenthood); the vocation to discipleship (Mt 4:18-22 & par.; Jn 1:37-51); the missionary vocation to Israel (Mt 10:5-7) and to the nations (Mt 28:18; Acts 9:15; 22:21; 26:17,18); Peter (Mt 16:18; 22:31); the diaconal vocation (Acts 6:3); Paul (Acts 9:1-19; Gal 1:11-24); the vocation of suffering (Mk 10:39 & par.; Acts 9:16); the martyr's vocation (Jn 21:18,19).

All these biblical vocations are related to the messianic vocation of Jesus, which was revealed at his baptism in the Jordan (Mt 3:13-17 & par.). His vocation was defined in terms of the depth of his divine sonship (Mt 3:17); his anointing by the Holy Spirit for mission, the mysterious program which was preannounced in the prophecies of the Servant of Yahweh (Is 42:1) and referred to by Jesus when he announced his passion (Mk 8:31; 9:30; 10:32 & par.).

In addition, Paul taught that there was a diversity of vocations and ministries (Rom 12:4-8; 1 Cor 12:4-11, 28-30); he distinguished between apostles, prophets, evangelists, pastors, and teachers (Eph 4:11). And one can summarize a good deal by noting that in Pauline theology, all vocations have to do with the work of the ministry and the building up of the body of Christ, so that we might attain the stature of Christ in all of its fullness (Eph 4:12-13).

With this group of texts in mind, let us attempt to discover some of the principal guidelines on vocation in the Bible.

A Biblical Profile of Vocation

First, in the Bible vocation is not the privilege of a single individual. Nor is it a distinction that ends in a particular person or group that has received a call (e.g., Abraham, Moses, the prophets, Mary, Paul, and even Jesus himself). Instead, vocation is a call to become involved in the process of mission. It is vocation for mission. It is a call to be sent.

Second, a vocation is never an imposition. There is a clear sense of human freedom in the response to the call to a vocation. Though we had no say in God's original act creating us, the call to mission requires our involvement, a conscious free response to God's call.

Third, vocation is not merely an ecstatic once and for all challenge, immovable and fixed in time. Instead, we are called to live all of our lives as life givers—God's call is a personalized invitation to each person by name. It is dynamic, open to change and to new understandings and growth, to maturation and self-transcendence.

Fourth, a specific call is not always clear. While God's call in itself is crystal clear, God usually doesn't explain the whys and the whats of the call. In many biblical calls there is, in fact, a sense in which the outcome of faith is veiled (Abraham, Mary, Paul; see Heb 11) and a dimension of partnership wherein God depends on the person whom God calls. God offers trust and support to that person, but also requires total loyalty (Israel, Peter, Paul).

Fifth, a vocation is not always linear or coherent in every aspect. We may experience comings and goings, advances and withdrawals. There are crises (Moses, Israel, the church). Human spiritual life is a dialectic process of progress, plateaus, and unhappy returns to such things as bad habits that may or may not lead to further and deeper positive conversions. At any given stage a call may be welcome or not welcome, and the tensions set up by the call can be intensely disorienting.

Sixth, vocation is not merely a function, a profession, or some kind of merely circumstantial or occasional employment. It requires total and often definitive commitment. We become fully caught up in it and in the networks of relationships that it encompasses. Because of this, vocations can require radical and total reorientations of personal and communal lifestyles.

Finally, God always calls us in the midst of specific historical contexts in which we or the group to which we belong find ourselves. God builds upon these factors. Yet every individual or group history is complex, because it has to do with prior histories assumed, not jettisoned in answering the call. These histories have various levels of meaning (consider, for example, the multiple meanings exegetes find in the biblical genealogies of Jesus). Nevertheless, history becomes personal and unique in every single person or community, society, culture, or people. God calls persons and communities who are unique and in whom many histories converge—family, culture, education and formation, social circumstance, tradition, and conflict. When God calls by name, the multiple dimensions of personality that make up the unique and mysterious reality of individual men, women, groups, and peoples are addressed.

Fundamental Attitudes to Vocation

When we acknowledge this biblical profile of vocations, we accept two fundamental attitudes. First, *faithfulness* to the past is involved. We are asked to look back to God's call. The prophets remind the people of God of the divine purpose. But this remembrance is dynamic. It does not become immobilized in the past. In the midst of change, it discovers new meanings of faithfulness that deepen and mature in the course of time. There will always be better ways of being and of responding to the divine call.

Second, *creativity* and *innovation*, both critical and prophetic, are involved. The Christian vocation is future-oriented, open to the unexpected, and free to be uprooted. This is the way in which charismatic "re-sourcing" works. It is always open to a better understanding and application of the source idea of vocation, in all of its richness and originality.

Faithfulness and creativity are criteria by which we can measure the quality of a vocation. Vocations move in tension between their origins and transformation. It is the same with individual persons and small groups and communities. The parable of the talents makes these criteria of Jesus very clear. The servants who were rewarded were those who brought together both faithfulness and creativity—and not him whose priority was faithfulness alone. This idea is developed in the gospels especially—the parables of the fig tree, the talents, and the sower that express the theme of fruitfulness and growth.

In the context of vocation for mission another emphasis emerges, especially our understanding of "otherness." The process is not merely intra-psychic. There is one who calls and sends and there are those who are called and are sent. This implies a love relationship. On the one hand, God chooses and accepts us just as we are, trusting us and sharing with us. Meanwhile, individual or groups are free to accept the divine call in faith and to commit themselves to it in love.

The Bible is clear in stating that, by whatever means and ways, it is always God who calls and sends us. God brings us to the certainty and knowledge that the Spirit is at work within us. God continues the mission of Jesus Christ in and through us. From the Bible we see that God expects from us certain decisive stands and attitudes:

Openness and docility: Vocation always involves a relationship between God and us. We experience vocation fully in our lives not merely as a function, but as feeling and loving—being and acting. In the religious life we rediscover this dimension in its deepest sense in the vow of chastity and in service to God and to our neighbor.

Attention to divine initiative: Vocation means responding to the plans and real will of God. We are not, nor can we ever be, in charge of the process. On our own we cannot measure the length and breadth of the divine plan. This fact relegates the delicate problem of internal and external authority to the church. In the particular realm of the religious life, the vow of obedience is implicit, with unavoidable implications for mission. At the same time, we must point to the constant need for discernment, whether in recognizing a vocation or call, or directing a vocation toward a specific mission endeavor.

Transparency to the Word: Underlying all of this is the need to bring our love into line with existential truth—that is to say, with what we truly are. Only in this way can we attain peace and foster a climate of open dialogue and of mutual acceptance. The Bible, above all the Sermon on the Mount (Mt 5-7), emphasizes that we have been called to truth, righteousness, and integrity at the most intimate and profound level of our beings. Jesus redefined sin from mere acts of lawlessness in regard to extrinsic commands to encompass our intentions and previous motivations—that is to say, the root causes of sin. A full-fledged morality is ultimately not abstract but is concretely rooted in existential truth. We must face up to the subtle processes that take place before we commit a sinful act. When we lack transparency and are not at peace with ourselves, we close up and become aggressive and defensive. In contrast, transparency allows us to act freely and consistently. It allows us to be challenged and converted, that is, to become conscious of who and what we are, a fact that is indispensable to the development of a mission vocation. If we want to see real growth in our lives, we will not become immobilized, nor will we absolutize what we are. We will not close ourselves within a static conformity, fearful of risk, burying our talents.

Coping with personal, existential truth is a fundamental precondition for the exercise of freedom. Such truth should not be confused with the speculative or abstract truth or the ideal of "pure knowledge," which often is mistaken as the root metaphor for knowledge in the Western tradition. The stuff of modern philosophy, abstract truth, has roots in ancient Greece, with significant contributions from medieval scholasticism and Cartesian rationalism. The entire postmodern movement is best explained as an ambiguous range of reactions against the pretenses of that ideal.

Becoming existentially truthful, on the other hand, brings what we are internally and externally in line with each other and in accord with what we can be. It requires that we not pretend to be other than what we are, that we not value ourselves above what we are. Applied to the religious life, this suggests an inherent dimension of the vow of poverty, as real as it is often overlooked. Poverty of spirit is a true existential qualification for voluntary poverty in mission.

Ultimately, God can call us by a direct act of the Spirit by inspiration, exhortation, through stimuli, and through our feelings and emotions. The divine call touches us personally in various life situations, in conditions that may be at one time more conducive than another to a favorable response. Prior awareness of these states of mind and spirit, which frequently happen during times of prayer, can prepare us to listen to the language of God. It can help us to understand progressively the ways in which the Lord communicates with us as persons and groups. More frequently, however, vocation comes to us through human intermediaries, both persons and institutions.

In addressing "vocations to religious life" we should keep two fundamental facts in mind. First, the vocation to be a religious does not presuppose an explicit call by the episcopal hierarchy, as is the case with the ordained ministerial vocation or with the lay vocation directed toward a specific pastoral ministry.

Second, neither does the religious vocation require a call by the superiors of religious orders. These superiors do, indeed, approve the candidates, once they have questioned and tested them and after providing them with competent and experienced assistance as candidates seek to discern their vocation. When they accept the candidates into their vocations, superiors are witnessing to the work of God in their lives. In God's name they recognize and accept the unique commitment to consecration that is expressed in each person's response. However, we should not forget that almost by definition, the religious vocation implies the free, mysterious interaction between God and the person who is confronted by a transcendent call. This unique character of the religious vocation requires that great care and wisdom be exercised by superiors in discerning the vocations. This rule applies to both admission to and dismissal from the congregation.

The Enigmas of Vocation

Borrowing from the language of mathematical proportionality, we could say that the apostles are to Paul what Israel is to the Gentiles; the elder son in the parable is to the prodigal son; Simon the Pharisee to the sinful woman; the Pharisees to Zacchaeus; and the scribes and doctors of the law to the man blind. Each of these cases is similar in the workings of the grace of vocation and in the divine initiative. Israel, the apostles, the elder son, Simon, and the Pharisees believed that they were related to God by bonds of privilege. Each was called by God to a vocation and to a specific kind of formation at some length. Similarly, God remained faithful to them and cared for them for even longer periods of time.

However, all the above were chosen by God despite their lack of discernible special qualifications. What immediately stands out in this is God's absolute gratuitousness, to which the subjects respond with enthusiasm and faithfulness. It becomes here very clear that vocations, conversion, and faithfulness, in fact, occur because of divine initiative and not by any voluntary and meritorious acquisition on our part. There is, thus, in the religious vocation a possible element of surprise. God can subvert the order of our criteria and expectations, of our hierarchy of values. God can gratuitously break into a person's life, as was done in the cases of St. Paul and St. Augustine, or in the lives of the "good thief" on the cross and of Mary Magdalene. This leads us to one ultimate criterion for our own actions in the process of discerning the vocations—*let us not hinder the surprises of a gracious God.*

It follows that for Christians—and especially for us who are religious—that our acceptance by God does not depend upon our own condition. It does not depend upon the way we understand faithfulness or on how we respond to the call to a vocation. Acceptance depends, instead and above all, on a divine initiative, which is as constant as it is unexpected. It is thus that the Lord makes himself known in our lives, independently of the frames of reference and signs of human endeavor. Every touch of vocation, conversion, or transformation seems to pass through some kind of gracious activity on the part of God. To these unexpected initiatives we must ever be alert. In this perspective, even our crises can be important moments in which God can act upon us. Our sins can become points of departure to a new life. In the case of Paul (Acts 26:9-18; see especially verses 16-18), we observe a radical transition from one vocation of grace (a faithful and militant Pharisee) to another (a tireless apostle). Paul calls this conversion a new creation, because there was nothing in him to justify this divine initiative (2 Cor 4:6; see 2:14-6:13).

Conclusion

The elements and principal features of the Christian vocation, as I have presented them, help us to understand the meaning of vocation to the religious and consecrated life and in relation to other Christian vocations. The biblical basis and guidelines that should shape our attitudes concerning vocation are a solid and accessible foundation to an elemental fact in our lives. We are called by God to life and to mission as an expression of God's love toward us. And we are also called as the result of that surprising affirmation of God's respect for our freedom and identity.

The call is personal and often communal. Whatever the case, our lives must be lived in the knowledge of the relationship between vocations, as well as their multiformity. They are not static and inert. As persons and members of communities, we will always be confronted, challenged and provoked with new situations, choices, and decisions. The permanent yes to the divine call must be reaffirmed continuously with ever new yeses. Our continuing affirmations must always be characterized by responsible acceptance of new eventualities—even of different expressions of the original vocations. Like mission, vocations are living and evolving realities. In them we can be affirmed and we can grow within the contexts of our personal and communal histories. The consecrated religious life is one of the forms of Christian vocation.

2

Directions

Mission, Evangelization, and Religious Vocations

The terms *mission* and *religious life* have each followed a peculiar theological course during the past thirty or forty years. Sometimes they have been tied together, but mostly they have been given distinct—and even reductionist and contradictory—meanings. Things went so far as to place the "contemplative" religious life in radical opposition to the "apostolic" or "active" religious life. The latter was closely tied to mission-as-outreach, while the former was confined to the interior salvation and perfection of individuals who had consecrated their lives to God. This implied that some vocations were apostolic and missionary vocations while others were not. This mistaken idea of apostolic religious life still persists in some countries where it is used exclusively for noncontemplative orders. Nonetheless, at a theological level the integral linking of every kind of religious life to mission is today universally accepted. The way in which to understand this relationship and how it works out is the topic of this chapter. But first I must make a semantic qualification. I propose to focus upon what it is in mission and in religious life that must be kept in mind at this stage of both our experience and understanding of the church and of theological reflection.

Defining Terms

In the recent historical context of theological reflection, of the practice of the church, and of the general understanding by Christians, the term *mission* has been generally tied to gospel proclamation and the planting of new churches in lands where peoples had not yet received the good news. In this regard, *mission* became *missions* in the plural, with the usual addition of the adjective *foreign*. Thus defined, mission connoted moving church persons, goods, and resources—both material and spiritual—with a view to effecting a profound change in the lifestyle and actions of the objects of mission. It further implied the substitution of Christian elements for a major portion of the indigenous cultures' symbolic structures and sociocultural paradigms with regard to analogous elements. All of this was understood and justified, of course, as entailed in the fundamental objective—to spread the gospel. Underlying all this was a defined and obligatory ecclesial model originally located in a such places as France, Italy, Spain, Germany, Holland, the United States, and Canada, which was to be replicated by new churches. This meaning of mission prevailed in the life of both Catholic and Protestant churches for the last five centuries. Religious congregations that communicated the gospel this way primarily were called "missionary" orders.

Less attention was given to the more theological and radical meaning of mission that has slowly gained ground in the post–Vatican Council II era. In terms that are both general and precise, we can say that mission is the universal and multiform irradiation of the free self-gift that God makes to humanity, in and through Jesus Christ. Jesus is central to a vital and active understanding of mission. Christian mission is nothing else than the ongoing unfolding of Jesus' mission in and through us. The mission of Jesus, then, inspires and strengthens us. By it we are renewed, and new ways and possibilities are made open for us.

The mission of Jesus, according to the gospel, turns on two interrelated axes. The first axis of mission is the revelation through Jesus of the eternal God who was first manifested to Israel. Jesus gives us a new and original perspective of God. Jesus lives and transmits a surprising relationship with God which is filial, intimate, and profound (Mt 11:25-27; Lk 10:20-22). He wants us also to have, in some measure, access to this relationship that we might live as adopted sons and daughters in fellowship with God and with one another.

The second axis of mission is the creation (or restoration) of a living community. Our freedom is renewed in a profound conversion experience, and we become fully open to God and to our brothers and sisters. It is a process of salvation, of redemption, and of integral liberation. This axis has two dimensions. First, Jesus takes on our humanity with all of its sins and limitations. He presents our need and our cry for forgiveness to God. At one and the same time he is the living expression and voice of the cries for justice of the suffering and oppressed peoples of every latitude and time. Jesus manifests himself above all as the living sacrament of reconciliation, toward God and toward us. Through Jesus, and by him alone, is sin—the evidence of our separation and severance from God—put to death in us. Through him and only by him do we see clearly the compassionate and merciful face of the God of Jesus Christ, who is also our God.

The second dimension reflects the fact that we human beings—who because of sin have distorted and destroyed the image of God in humanity, a humanity created for joyful fellowship with God and with one another—have become actively associated with God in the reconstruction of a world of love and truth, freedom and justice, solidarity and fellowship. Jesus shares with us the responsibility for creating a new history, where life reigns supreme and where the signs of the Kingdom become visible. Jesus entrusts us with this mission and sends us forth to make disciples of all nations (Mt 28:18-20 & par.). He makes us participants and coworkers with him in this mission through the empowerment of the Holy Spirit. He calls us to mission within a community that he has willed unto faith—the church.

Thus, the mission of the church—and our mission—is to continue to manifest this twofold mission of Christ in the power of the Spirit. Mission is to make the God of Jesus Christ fully known to all humanity. When we allow ourselves to be liberated by Jesus, we become participants in his liberation for every human being, and we enter into creative community with God and with one another. This new community is empowered to transform our histories of death into histories of life, the consummation of which shall be fullness of life.

This, then, is mission, according to current biblical and theological understandings, which retrieve a horizon more radical and all-encompassing than the previous mission concept. This mission is entrusted to all Christians by virtue of baptism. Through baptism we are grafted to Jesus the Christ, we share in his life, and we are both called and sent. Our mission involvement does not depend upon how old we are or where we live. Mission in this perspective becomes the heart and soul of all of our activity and communication. In fact, theologically speaking, mission only has meaning when we can look beyond functionality and efficiency. If this is so, missioners are not wholly dependent upon human mediations and activities, instruments and methods.

It is not dualism to distinguish between being and acting. Nor do we give primacy to the former, as if being were the whole of mission. Rather, we need to understand that *being-in-mission* becomes evident, spontaneously and coherently, wherever the doing and acting of mission are dynamically and synergistically interrelated. For this reason, being-in-mission requires flexibility. In point of fact, being-in-mission in real life contexts—which by definition are constantly changing—is the inspiration of mission praxis. This praxis—constantly evaluated in the light of its applicability to concrete situations—is what gives shape to the identity of being-in-mission. This is the case whatever our personal or community vocation within the church in each context.

Therefore, mission can no longer be used to imply transplanted or foreign context churches. Mission does not necessarily go hand in hand with "civilization," where the host culture must accept the missionary's sociocultural paradigm. This is not a criterion for successful evangelization. Authentic mission is not ethnocentric; it does not impose or absolutize the culture of the sending church. Nor does it demand the loss of the cultural identity of the evangelized. Neither does mission, however, grant a privileged status to the host culture, preserving it unchanged, inert, and alienated—in hibernation as it were—isolated from the relational and transformational processes of life.

Mission presupposes and implies the recognition of the potential universality of Jesus' gospel of salvation-as-liberation, which bursts the boundaries of time and space. The gospel addresses every human being, every culture and society. It speaks to all people as they are, in their own contexts, with all of their potential for good, with the potential of being impregnated, transformed, and empowered from within by the gospel. The God of Jesus Christ is the God of all. In ways that may be quite different from our understanding, this God lives and acts in the lives of all peoples. God is revealed in the multiple interaction of the unique histories of every people. The created world, as it is constantly being transformed by its inhabitants, is the stuff that God cherishes and liberates with us as coworkers. Taken as a whole, then, this history is the history of salvation.

We move, therefore, from a more restrictive and functional concept of mission—as a limited action of a few (the "missionaries") and a few local churches (the "sending churches")—to a broader and more integrated view. Mission belongs to all of us in the church; it is lived and practiced in the mutual interaction of peoples and churches. The poor are evangelized, and they evangelize as well. The evangelizing church is also evangelized.

In the context of this fundamental vocation of every Christian—a vocation that is intimately tied to mission as an indivisible whole and as the fundamental orientation of our lives—we can now focus on the meaning for us today of the consecrated religious and apostolic life.

Consecrated Religious Life

What distinguishes consecrated religious life among the various forms of life and vocations in the church? Said briefly, the primary distinguishing factor is one's *public commitment, recognized and legitimized by the church, to seek consistently and radically to live the evangelical "project" according to the rule of life of a given community as a primary goal of one's life*. This radical translation of the presence of Christ in the world must reproduce in the one answering the call and in the religious community the twofold dimension of the life and mission of Jesus. At stake are the following:

- *An intimate and loving relationship with the living God, when we fully accept the free gift of divine love* . . .
  This loving relationship between God and those who are called to consecrated life must be lived with the same kind of intense commitment as a marriage relationship, wherein man and woman become the living sacrament of God's love, individually and together. This manifestation of God is accomplished through a diversity of vocations. All consecrated persons have the special task of sharing the gift that they have received so that it might multiply. In sum, we affirm the multiple forms in which mission is activated by means of innumerable mediations and with virtually no boundaries.

- *With particular attention to simple folk and to the disadvantaged* (Mt 11:25-27; Lk 4:16-22; 7:18-23), especially to those who are hindered from establishing a loving relationship with God because of perversions in their societies and cultures, particularly because of the kind of suffering that dehumanizes and debases people. Is this not the tragic condition of the major portion of humanity today? Mission-as-liberation is, therefore, all the more imperative, because every person must have free access to the liberating God who is made known in Jesus. At the same time mission must overcome everything that hinders, restricts, oppresses, and limits freedom of choice in individual persons and in sociocultural groups. A very important dimension of liberation-as-inculturation of the gospel in the evangelization process is to free people from complex social and cultural restraints. This aspect of mission is an expression and demonstration of the continuity of our mission with the mission of Jesus Christ, especially in his service to people in need.

From this dual perspective, religious life is not superior to other vocations. It does not have its own exclusive sphere of action which is inaccessible to other vocations. Religious life cannot be absent or distant from the world, or indifferent to its problems.

In similar fashion, consecrated life can no longer be reduced to a choreography of symbols or to standardized ways of acting, dressing, communicating, speaking, and ritualizing behavior. We are aware today that this symbolic apparatus and ritual, which can be precisely dated, improperly became the primary characteristic of the religious life. In that deformation of the ideal, a body of static concepts and ways of proceeding came to be universally identified as the authentic meaning of consecration in religious life. And, for a very long time, this approach to the religious vocations remained untouchable, in concept as well as practice.

We now affirm that consecrated, apostolic religious life is a public commitment and profession, before God, the church, and the world, to follow Jesus Christ in community at whatever cost (Mt 25:31-46; Lk 10:29-37). We all have the potential to do this, by the gift of faith and the grace of baptism. But the consecrated life is realized when we respond freely and consciously—in various ways and diverse temporal-spatial contexts—to the call to Christian mission in the world.

This vision of the consecrated religious life is of necessity *christo-logical*. As we have seen, it can only be understood when Jesus Christ and his mission are the point of departure. But, furthermore, this is an *ecclesiological* concept, because religious life can only be expressed and legitimized within an ecclesial context. This is, in fact, one of the possible forms of religious presence and action of the church in the world. This means that the religious life is neither a private enterprise of a person or group nor an end in itself, concerned only with the needs of the persons enlisted in a given religious community.

The christological and ecclesiological dimensions are oriented, there-fore, toward mission. Mission gets to the very root and primary mean-ing of the divine plan, whether it relates to the saving reality of Jesus Christ, crucified and resurrected, or to the apostolic nature of the church. Therefore, at the heart of our understanding and justification for the religious life, in whatever form, is mission.

Religious life is missionary because of the inherent radicality of its commitment to God and to the church. Religious participate directly in a dynamic dimension of mission—making known the full and inexhaust-ible message and mystery of Jesus Christ. The role of religious is to pass the message on to the lives of people and to the structures of cul-ture and society. This includes every form of consecrated religious life, whether active or contemplative. Both are apostolic and missionary, within the radical theological definition that I am using.

To put it more precisely, mission transcends the religious life and can even do without it. But without mission the religious life has neither meaning nor reason for being. Let us now consider the relationship be-tween both and its consequences.

Mission and Evangelization

In the synagogue of Nazareth (Lk 4:16-22), with reference to the text in Isaiah (61:1,2), Jesus explains his mission fully and succinctly—*to evangelize*. When he responds to the disciples of John the Baptist, Jesus defines his identity in terms of mission (Lk 7:18-23). Concluding his mission on earth, Jesus calls the apostles, and those that will come after them, and sends them to the ends of the earth to evangelize, to give continuity to the mission that he initiated among the people of Israel (Mt 28:18-20; Mk 16:15; Lk 24:47,48; Jn 20:21,22; Ac 1:8). Paul, whom God made an apostle, underlines the responsibility of his mission, which is to evangelize (Rom 15:16; 1 Cor 10:17).

We can say, then, that mission and evangelization are related. We need to bring these terms together once more, after too long a separation. The reason for this divorce was twofold. On the one hand, mission has been defined too functionally and restrictively, as we have seen. On the other hand, evangelization has had too narrow a focus—limited primarily to the announcement or proclamation of the gospel message.

An in-depth reading of the gospel in the light of the evangelizing mission of Jesus, which I have touched upon, makes one point clear. Evangelization, while it is the concrete expression of mission, has a broader and more comprehensive meaning. It is only in this context, it seems to me, that we can capture the meaning and the role of religious life in relation to mission.

In order to make my point clearer, it may help to group the specific dimensions of the evangelization process around four verbs. Together, these verbs translate mission and evangelization according to scripture and tradition—and in particular in Jesus, in Paul, and in the early church. I am not using these verbs necessarily in the chronological order in which they have developed, but in a logical sequence that, as we shall see, will help to clarify and affirm the evangelization process.

Dynamic Development of the Evangelization Process

To Witness

The first active dimension of evangelization is to witness, that is, to affirm by what we are, what we believe, know, and live for. It means being a witness and giving witness. Our witness may not necessarily eventuate in death. But in every witness that we give in adverse circumstances there is a conscious acceptance of possible martyrdom, moral and/or physical. In mission, which is to evangelize, we are always called to witness. We are called to express in our lives the content of our faith, our adhesion by faith to the God of Jesus Christ and to the ethical implications of this faith. Faith convictions reflect sound ethics and coherent lives. In many parts of the world and in not a few social environments there is no other way to evangelize today, since the gospel can often only be *lived* by the evangelizers, *not proclaimed*, because of a hostile geographical, cultural, political, or religious environment where a verbal witness or an institutional presence of the church is impossible.

These contexts aside, beyond merely being witnesses we must in fact have the courage to give witness. Without a doubt Peter was one of the more qualified witnesses of Jesus. But in the hour of great testing Peter not only did not witness, he denied Jesus three times. We may not have to pay the price of suffering for our witness as was common in the early history of Christianity, or recently in militantly atheistic political systems. Indeed, the very milieu of indifferent agnosticism in modern society often undermines the vitality of our witness. We can live in the silent and cowardly accommodation of opportunistic convenience.

To Serve

The second active dimension of evangelization is to serve. We can be pragmatic about our service, going about it professionally and functionally, as technicians who choose that which works best. We can serve with a top-down philanthropic attitude, as those who give out of their abundance with a sense of paternalism, who help without transforming. In and of themselves such attitudes can perhaps make life more human, but they are not evangelization. Jesus insisted that he came to serve. But his service was a constant giving of himself to others; he became involved in their welfare so as to liberate them and help them to grow. Evangelical service is to know and support the just causes in which the people that we serve are struggling. To serve is to commit oneself to them. Christian service, then, is a form of love which flows out from us, enveloping others creatively and freely. It is like the love of God.

To Communicate

The third active dimension of evangelization is to communicate. In current usage, *to communicate* is a transitive verb that denotes passing on to others knowledge and information. *To communicate in evangelization, however, is above all to put oneself in dialogue with someone else.* Christian communication asks us to give up monologues. It requires us to get close to those with whom we are communicating and to allow them to be themselves, as much as we demand authenticity from ourselves. True communication does not take place without an attitude of respect for the truth of those with whom we are communicating. Mutual transparency is very difficult to achieve in daily life. But when practiced it can reveal the points of agreement and inevitable disagreement between us, enabling us to work out our differences together. When we communicate in this way we make communion between ourselves possible, as well as communion with God as self-revealed to us. Can there be authentic evangelization when the conditions for communication are lacking?

To Share

The fourth active dimension of evangelization is to share what one has with others, to give wholly to the very depths of one's being. It is to make what we have received available to others; to open up for others opportunities that might otherwise remain closed to them. Evangelizers give of themselves as Jesus gave himself for us. He gave his life for those he loved (Jn 15:13), the ultimate proof of the love which he taught. This definition of evangelization connotes losing one's life in order to gain lives (other lives and our own as well, with a new vision). Evangelization on these terms is rooted in truth and grace. It presupposes full respect for others and recognition of their freedom, all the while eschewing any sort of imposition, and any expectation of reward or return by the evangelizer. It is a project of complete gratuity. It is thus that God shared with us the gift of his only Son, and that Jesus freely revealed to us the uniqueness of his God. From this revelation his mission proceeds.

The Path of Faith in Evangelization

There is an internal logic in the above four verbs. By definition they are forms of evangelization, ways in which the fundamental content of the gospel is made known even before it is formally proclaimed by the spoken word. The actions these verbs connote are in and of themselves part of the process of evangelization. But above all, there is a coherent thread that runs through them, the same kind of logic that is implicit in the Sermon on the Mount. What these verbs signify and the actions that they imply impart credibility to the announcement. Evangelization is the work of the Spirit. The Spirit can work through us in spite of ourselves and does not need our assent to work through us.

Nevertheless, in light of the gospel and Jesus' attitude to the Pharisees, and the way in which he taught the apostles, it is difficult to conceive of the announcement without the support of witness, service, communication, and sharing.

Proclamation is central in evangelization. The church has always understood this to be true. The evangelizer must proclaim the gift that is granted by God in and through Jesus Christ. Knowledge of this gift makes us receptive to the liberating action of this transcendent and yet immanent, ever-present God. By God's self-gift we are introduced into an economy of free salvation unattainable by our own efforts. Along with the gift of Jesus Christ, the evangelizer must also announce the "news" of the gospel. This novelty is expressed above all and always through a fresh realization of the interrelationship of God and of humanity. Furthermore, the gospel announcement "re-presents" relationships between human beings and God in new light and redirects the relationship between humanity and nature (the realm of ecology). This is not the place to detail the content of the above affirmations. We must, however, remind ourselves that Jesus introduced a new vision and uniquely creative paradigms in each of these dimensions. The person, mystery, and message of Jesus Christ as gift and good news constitute the fundamental core of the announcement in evangelization.

The proclamation of the gospel always makes a claim on us. It is never neutral or conformist. The gospel shakes up people and societies. It questions attitudes, denounces unjust situations, makes demands of us at the very depths of our being—calling us to change our hearts, transform our lives, and take new directions. Concrete faith may lead us to question, to denounce, and even to confront what is taken to be normal by the world in which we live. Along the way we will become aware of the dichotomies, contradictions, ambiguities, complicities, and ideologies—disguised or submerged—that are present in the way in which we express our faith and live our lives. We face new challenges that can thrust the gospel forward with new emphases. Inherent to confrontation in the gospel is the prophetic dimension of evangelization.

The principal consequence, however, of evangelization as confrontation is the process of transformation that it sets in motion. Both individual persons and social groups are transformed in evangelization. Because the personal and social dimensions interact it is difficult to define which precedes or generates the other. What does come first: personal conversion or social and structural transformation? In fact, there is cross-fertilization. Holistic evangelization must see to both, avoiding the extremes of mere interior piety or outward activism. Conversion and liberation are integral parts of the evangelization process. They are also the greatest fruit and final product of evangelization.

A perspective of growth opens up for us in lives that are transformed by faith. Growth is inherent to evangelization because it opens us up to a double transcendence: 1) in personal, human development *as subjects of our own history*; and 2) in growth in *eschatological orientation toward the wholly Other*. Jesus expressed this broad anthropological and theological understanding of growth in several parables—above all in the parables of the Kingdom and the talents. Jesus himself transformed his disciples through his life, his teaching, his death. But it was his resurrection, the gift of a new life, that brought the Spirit. This is the key factor in conversion, liberation, and growth. The Holy Spirit is the very soul of evangelization. The Spirit is evangelization's primary inspiration through the understanding that the Spirit gives us of the linkage (provided by the Spirit) between what and where we are and the fundamental reference point, Jesus Christ.

Vocation for Mission and the Missionary Vocation

It is crucial that the creative power of the pascal mystery of Jesus Christ become active in evangelization through the Holy Spirit. It must empower us to go in mission to the ends of the earth to witness and to serve, to communicate and to share, to announce, to make a claim on, and to transform. This is our Christian mission. It is this that gives meaning and a sense of responsibility to us as men and women religious. And this is particularly true in our case, because of what we are and the vocation that we profess. This mission vision shall remain, therefore, in our lives, whatever the paths and the happenstances, and whichever instruments and methods we use in our missionary presence and action. In all of this we should remain completely free to be faithful and creative in our vocation to mission.

Among the many versions and contexts of the religious life in orders and congregations, some religious communities presume that mission and evangelization have a unique priority. They define themselves explicitly as missionary. It is not the case, though, that mission belongs exclusively to them. Rather, that they are uniquely inspired by a priority understanding of evangelization, in the terms already defined. Mission and evangelization are the points of reference and the criteria for discernment and self-evaluation of every aspect of their being, doing, and communicating in both their individual and corporate exercise of religious life.

Understanding of the explicitly missionary identity of some religious institutes is important for the church. This acts constantly as a kind of prophetic reminder of where ecclesial mission should be heading. When those in the missionary vocations, both religious and lay, shoulder responsibility for the mission of bearing the good news to every nation, they help draw people together. They contribute to knowledge, diversification, and enrichment concerning cultures and faith communities. At a time when Catholicism is updating itself, missionary thought and self-understanding are more aware of other religious traditions and are clearly moving with attitudes of mutual respect into interreligious dialogue. Thus dialogue becomes a process of mutual illumination concerning the mysterious action of God among the nations. This approach to mission requires a complete renewal of education and formation within missionary congregations.

The universality of mission, which is the immediate consequence of faith and baptism for *all* Christians, is not opposed to the specific missionary vocation of the *few* who embrace religious life, with its special requirements, preparation, and specialized training. In the same way, the unique vocation of the prophets did not clash with the fundamental vocation of the people of Israel. On the contrary, the prophetic vocation served to purify, give feedback to, and reorient a people confused by the harsh hand that God and history had seemingly dealt to Israel.

I wish to suggest that globalization and the growing positive affirmation of identity on the part of many cultures, rather than indicating the need to close down missionary religious life, offer promising opportunities and new challenges for missionary institutes. Keeping in mind their respective histories and wealth of experience, missionary groups should step out in faith to build a different future. They have not been sent to recover or restore a glorious past. Instead, a world that is undergoing profound sociocultural transformations requires new institutions. This certainly and unavoidably calls for creative change in the church. Something like what John Paul II calls "new evangelization" must take place. This will require passion, new expressions, and new methods. But it also implies a new approach to classic truths and a new capacity to communicate them in such a different, complex world. It is important to realize this, especially when we face the challenge of communicating the gospel ethically, at the personal and individual level, and to entire societies, cultures, and nations.

3

Mission, Apostolate, and Pastoral Ministry

The Encounter of Religious Life
and Evangelizing Activity

In the previous chapter we emphasized the meaning and range of mission as it relates to evangelization from the perspective of consecrated life. In this chapter, we shall try to illuminate an important distinction for religious life in relation to evangelizing action. In this connection people normally use three terms interchangeably—the noun *apostolate*, the adjective *apostolic*, and *pastoral*, which in Latin languages is used both as adjective and noun. It is, however, good to remember that, while the apostolate can express itself in a pastoral approach to mission, and while pastoral activity and planning always presupposes an apostolic outlook, there are differences between them that go beyond mere shades of meaning. We must be precise in our definitions.

Pastoral Action

The term *pastoral action* (*pastoral* as a noun in Portuguese) suggests a bringing together of goals and projects which have their source and direction in the pastor. Pastoral action thus understood becomes a reality through the agency of evangelizers at every level of the church—local, regional, national, continental, and worldwide. There can therefore be different levels of pastoral inspiration and action.

The entire Catholic church, through the agency of the pope, can shape its pastoral activity at a worldwide level, and this will have broad influence in every country and the various local churches (dioceses). Pope Pius XI, for example, initiated Catholic Action in the 1930s and 1940s. Catholic Action adapted and expressed itself variously in such places as

Italy, France, and Belgium, countries which in turn inspired new forms of lay pastoral action in Argentina and Brazil. In the United States and Germany, however, a different style of local church had long been established, and Catholic Action adapted itself to that structure, even while it strengthened these prior experiences of lay pastoral action.

John Paul II has made a worldwide impact upon pastoral activity by emphasizing the dimension of culture as it relates to faith and by encouraging local churches to involve themselves in a "new evangelization." The meetings of episcopal conferences at Medellín and Puebla were decisive and productive for the pastoral orientation of the church in Latin America, because they opened up a pastoral approach that involved the entire church in Latin America during the decades of the '70s and '80s.

The axis of this model of pastoral activity was the evangelical, solidary, and prophetic preferential option for the poor. The major consequences of this approach were the special attention that was given to the reality in which people, in particular the marginalized and oppressed, live. This became the indispensable reference point in interpreting the Bible and theological reflection. It is the source of the Latin American church's awareness of the need for transformation and justice in order to nourish a faith that is engaged with life and ethically expressed.

The National Conference of Bishops of Brazil voted, in April of 1991, a beautiful and compact general objective for the pastoral action of that national church. These objectives were later applied regionally and locally throughout Brazil, in response to the specific needs of the people of God in each ecclesial context.

We have said that in Latin America the word *pastoral* has a double connotation. First, it links the church's evangelizing action and its shepherds, including the bishops and the pope. Second, pastoral action takes shape through an organization and coordination of persons and groups— such as associations and movements, and ecclesial communities and institutions—at both the local and international levels. One of the recent characteristics of religious life in Latin America has been the growing presence of religious in the church's pastoral inspiration and implementation at every level. The document *Mutuae Relationes* dealt in depth with this correlation between shepherds and the religious.

Apostolate

The term *apostolate* is broader in scope than *pastoral action*. *Apostolate*—the dynamic theological expression of faith, hope, and love—embraces multiple forms of making Christian identity concrete and active. It is marked by spontaneously sharing, consciously or unconsciously, the presence and action of the Holy Spirit in and through us. The apostolate deepens in us the relationship between Jesus and his apostles, provided that we are in him, and is the mission to which the apostles were called and which the gospels recount. The apostles were sent to share and establish this same relationship with many others: vocation and mission, vocation for mission. The apostolate is the full and constant action of the God of Jesus Christ. It becomes the evidence of God's free gift of self to and through us for salvation and liberation. The apostolate, then, is the specific translation of mission, in the sense that mission was set forth in the previous chapter.

Pastoral action can be one of the channels through which the apostolate is joined to every level of the church. The apostolate, however, can transcend specific pastoral activities. The apostolate flows directly from a coherent and productive expression—which is both theological and ethical—of Christian faith and life. To limit the apostolic presence and life to explicit pastoral activity impermissibly reduces and impoverishes mission. It defines apostolate in merely sociological (human and institutional) categories. It limits the Holy Spirit's surprising, unexpected, and inexhaustible work in persons and human communities.

Each person is an apostle in his or her way. Farmers or laborers, teachers or lawyers, for example, may settle with their families in a city. Even before they make contact with the local church they are potential apostles to the degree that their faith, enabled by the sacraments of baptism and confirmation, shines forth. They are apostles on the strength of their lay vocational identification with the mission of church. They are apostles when they live their personal, family, professional, and work lives in harmony with their basic Christian beliefs, even if they belong to no formal pastoral organization. This is the case with the great majority of believers and professing members of the church. Take another example. A Catholic university is apostolic when it maintains a clear relationship among research, teaching, knowledge, and its role as servant to humanity in light of the gospel.

Workers, teachers, and lawyers, as well as Catholic universities, may, however, not be directly connected with the pastoral action of a particular church. This does not make them necessarily any less apostolic or less engaged in evangelization. Or the above entities could, in due time, become actively involved in the pastoral action of their church. Their engagement in some form of apostolate and evangelizing mission will make them aware of their role in a coordinated apostolate, under the guidance, leadership, and evaluation of a pastor. This kind of involvement in solidarity with other Christians may disseminate a dimension of apostolicity to communities and movements which may be individualistic and lacking in pastoral awareness.

Religious Life, Apostolate, and Pastoral Action

Lumen Gentium (the Vatican Council II constitution on the nature of the church) was one of the principal documents of the Council. It made it quite clear that religious vocations are not in and of themselves part of the hierarchical structure of the church. Religious, as religious, neither initiate nor carry on pastoral action, but they are often appointed to pastoral and apostolic tasks in local churches by bishops and internationally by the Holy Father. In its strictest sense, religious life is one of many public vocations and, by definition, the vows and community life of a given institute of religious life must be recognized and validated by church authority. Thus religious orders are under the jurisdiction of a pastor. As such, they may be juridically enrolled in pastoral activities of the church in fulfillment of their particular call.

From historical and juridical points of view, however, various forms of religious life have arisen in the church and have offered new and different lifestyles endowed with, for example, charismatic and prophetic dimensions. Indeed, emerging forms of religious life have been and should continue to be living apostolic forces. Rather than define themselves in terms of a specific pastoral objective, religious communities have a more extensive apostolic brief that can on occasion assume a particular pastoral agenda (for example, the apostolate of the press or health care). In carrying out these agenda, religious—along with other vocations—encourage and enrich the church. With their apostolic vision, religious can pioneer new, unofficial pastoral perspectives. They can serve also as a force for renewing pastoral programs at any level.

A case in point is the way St. Francis of Assisi and his friars introduced a new approach to preaching the gospel within the medieval urban milieu. This new focus, translated into a particular way of living and manner of work, was quite different from the then-dominant rural monastic model. While monks settled in fixed monasteries to which the faithful came, Franciscans moved among the people, deeply touched by the spiritual and material needs of those they sought to serve. The creation of funds for widows (a kind of early private social security) for example, came about because of the friars' awareness of specific needs of the people in the new urban situation created by new modes of commerce and social life in the Middle Ages. From this apostolic matrix—which the Dominicans, the Servites, and the Hermits of St. Augustine emulated—emerged a new paradigm of religious life. The followers of the mendicant paradigm were orders that adhered to a conventual, but not monastic, religious life. When recognized by the church, the mendicant model produced multiple forms of pastoral action, some of which have lasted until today.

In contrast with the isolated apostolate of a laborer, teacher, or lawyer moving into a new area (the example of a lay apostolate given above), religious life is marked by a corporate community dimension. A religious order or congregation is, above all, an apostolic body—even before it receives official ecclesiastical recognition or finds a particular pastoral expression. As religious go about their apostolic business, they must be attentive to particular situations and pastoral options of the dioceses or regions of the church where they intend to operate. In this way a religious institute can insert itself vitally and prophetically into pastoral contexts in ways that contribute to the development of the pastoral action of the church, while respecting the diversity of vocations.

It follows that religious life has great potential for mission presence and involvement around the world. Religious communities can be much more flexible and are potentially even more universal than the local church in which they work. The local church, which is institutional, territorial, and programmatic, is often limited in its flexibility. Because they relate directly to an evangelical project but are not intrinsically a part of the hierarchical structure of the church, religious can be more open and adaptable. In fact, this is what we see down through history—multiple, diverse, parachurch expressions of Christian concern that are molded into new paradigms, each with a variety of apostolic possibilities. Indeed, congregations founded in response to one geographical or ecclesial challenge have often found themselves moving into a wider international theater.

Understanding Pastoral-Apostolic Mission
for Western Religious Life

In our day, religious institutes are faced with the problem of basic convergence—within their respective charisms—in their interpretation and understanding of the radical demands of the gospel. But unity must inescapably be expressed in diversity, and gospel radicality in a variety of apostolic and pastoral modalities. As we shall see in the next chapter (on the inculturation of their orders' charisms), religious institutes should not make absolute their original forms and ways of being, acting, and communicating. They must avoid attempting to reproduce the sociocultural context of their founders or acting merely to please a majority of their present membership. To the contrary, religious institutes should be encouraged to develop new forms, forms that may be alien to the dominant culture, particularly the culture of Europe and North America. Similarly, the enormous impact of the presence of the poor must be a determining factor in bringing about an evangelical, apostolic, and pastoral radicality in the non-Western or Third World. A sound inculturation of the religious life must take this fact very much into account.

Without a doubt, religious life, born in the East, took root, matured, and flourished extraordinarily in the West, particularly in the Mediterranean region. There have been, on the one hand, tremendous changes in the paradigms of religious life over time—the monks, mendicants, regular canons and clerics, lay fraternities and sisterhoods, and action-oriented institutes for education, health, and social aid, not to mention the great variety of contemplative lifestyles. On the other hand, there have been significant examples of religious inertia.

Such was the case, for example, with the women's religious orders in general. Over several centuries, while the male orders developed and established numerous forms of flourishing religious life, the women's orders, including branches of male orders, were forced to maintain homogeneous and static manners of life and limits on expressing their diverse charisms. Until recently, such matters as claustral confinement versus external relationships in women's communities were determined by monastic usages rather than by apostolic approaches.

Nevertheless, the possibilities for new manifestations and forms of religious life are not exhausted. To deny this is to lack historical perspective and sensitivity to the inexhaustible workings of the Spirit. We cannot limit religious consecration to ancient forms (whether conserved or restored), to recently created modes, or to embryonic projects of the future. None of the forms of living the religious life is unique, immutable, or irreversible. However significant or meaningful the contributions and wisdom of the past may seem, there is no justification for saying that this or that form of religious life is obligatory for the entire church.

The Emergence of Cultural and Religious Diversity

We must take seriously the emergence of cultural and religious diversity. Freed from ethnocentric Western notions of cultural superiority, we can begin to appreciate the new opportunities that are opening up for the church in diverse historical, cultural, and geographical contexts. In many such places the church is already present in the middle of the cultural ferment. It got there, however, as a foreign element, by coming from the outside with an approach to evangelization that was quite homogeneous, unified, and uniform. Today we are better able to perceive other possibilities and differences that could have occurred in the encounter with these cultures. In fact, though, despite what could have occurred, Latin America, Africa, and Asia have only begun to offer their original and specific contributions to religious life with foci as much pastoral as apostolic.

In Latin America, specifically, being consistent with the preferential option for the poor has had three major consequences.

1. *The presence of religious—above all women—among the poor, in barrios, favelas, and other marginal neighborhoods, in what we call "insertion."* The impact of being close to the people has impressed upon religious a feeling of instability, a yearning for simplicity, a sense of commitment and, above all, a real awareness of the great urgency of the challenge. We begin to perceive firsthand the problems, anguish, and frustrations of marginalized peoples. We discover evidence of the perverse activities of the mechanisms of oppression: the discrimination and marginalization of the poor, under many guises; all of this and much more. As we reflect upon the meaning of poverty—the need to connect discourse to life and to be sensitive to the soul of the poor, in the religious dimension above all—we are being moved to reinterpret and reorder the religious life. Admittedly, there have been tensions and failures. Here and there mission was entrusted to the wrong persons, or to those who were perhaps insufficiently trained for the task. And we may have overstated our engagement in secular, political, and labor movements. While all of this may be true, none of it can gainsay an evident fact: a new way of living the religious life is beginning to appear. Again, this is only one form of vocation among many, and it would be disingenuous to pretend otherwise. Nonetheless, one cannot exaggerate the contribution of the option for the poor to improving religious life. Religious life, we see, can become more evangelically radical and more actively ethical.

2. *Insight—especially among women's orders—into the importance of linking the global question of feminism to the process of women's full liberation, in particular the liberation of poor women.* This has been both an inspiration and an important result of the insertion process. First of all, an observation. Throughout Latin America the presuppositions of first-world (and in particular of North American) feminism are gaining ground. But it must be said that this kind of feminism is based more upon Western liberal traditions than indigenous dynamics. Such feminism claims for women the same individual rights and access to power, opportunities, and jobs that men have. The great majority of Latin American women consider this feminist agenda rather reductionist. Instead of a frequent attitude of unbending confrontation with men, the insertion of Latin American women into new situations has demonstrated an emphatic level of engagement with others, sensitivity to difference and diversity. This new kind of perception leading to another type of commitment is the natural consequence of discovering inhuman levels of poverty and misery in this continent. That reality affects both men and

women, as well as millions of children, all of them painfully excluded. Unmasked are those masses excluded from social, economic, and political life. Bereft of any civic or religious involvement, these masses wander in cities and over countryside. They lack personal identity and the hope of survival. Among these so-called throw-away people, the presence of women is tragic. A question becomes inescapable: Are they being overlooked by the church's preferential option for the poor?

3. *New awareness and personal experience of ancient spiritual traditions.* I refer to the renewal, and sometimes, perhaps, the re-creation, of indigenous spirituality. To be faithful to their fundamental tenets, the spirituality of the religious orders must now attempt to respond more appropriately—in focus, expression, and practice—to the cultural sensibilities and social needs found in emerging sociocultural areas. The people, and with them religious, are becoming ever more aware of the uniqueness of each area. Their presence has either been overlooked or suppressed for many years. Such is the case with the Afro-American communities in Brazil and the Caribbean and the numerous indigenous peoples that are scattered throughout Latin America. Awareness is slowly growing concerning each of these cultural groups.

Grappling with the Distinction between the Apostolate of Communities and Pastoral Action

During the current transformation of the religious life, it is important to distinguish clearly between the apostolate of a given religious community and pastoral activity and planning in a given area. This distinction is necessary in order better to define the evangelizing mission of the numerous religious congregations and orders. On this distinction lies the theological justification for the relative freedom of prophetic and charismatic action by religious, as well as for evaluating the discernment of religious groups concerning what apostolic missions they should undertake.

Religious institutes must, above all, deepen their apostolic inspiration—that is, sharpen the understanding of their particular call. Their primary evangelical project should mesh with the founder's charismatic vision and its historical development. This should shape the order's apostolic profile, even as it hones the criteria for possible involvement in the variety of possible pastoral activities the order may consider.

The contribution of religious institutes to pastoral action should be determined by whether their apostolic vision meshes with a particular pastoral need, not the contrary. Said another way, sharpening their criteria for properly inserting themselves into concrete dimensions of the apostolate can help a religious order better evaluate episcopal invitations to undertake pastoral activities in particular regions, countries, or dioceses. Religious institutes need this same apostolic discernment to distinguish between pastoral practices and spiritual emphases when several orders are working in the same geographical area or diocese. Present-day pastoral planning cannot afford to impose uniform pastoral practices upon different orders working in the same area. The fact that religious are at the service of the church should not be used as a basis for filling vacancies and meeting pastoral needs without first taking into account the differences between the charisms of diverse religious orders. Instead, good planning should take into account the diversity, complementarity, and pastoral subsidiarity that comprise the unique apostolic identities of the congregations—in themselves and as they relate to the other church vocations.

To summarize, religious communities, both male and female, should not be pushed into filling vacancies and taking up pastoral responsibilities that are incompatible with their vocations. This saps the church's charismatic energies. It denies the multiplicity of gifts of the Spirit and the plurality of services available to the people of God.

Bishops, Religious, and Pastoral Priorities

Bishops should be encouraged to act with pastoral concern for religious orders by helping them to remain faithful to their particular goals. Bishops must also be evenhanded in balancing their response to the immediate practical needs of the diocese and the need for religious communities to maintain apostolic creativity. By way of example, soon after Vatican II there were occasional—and mercifully, brief—plans by bishops to curtail the international vocation of several orders by making them respond more directly to the needs of the dioceses, under the direct supervision of the bishops. The results were tragic for both local and international mission. Once the religious of that generation were exhausted, there were no men or women to replace them, either from other congregations or from among diocesan priests. This kind of attempt is contrary to the global missionary vocation of the church. The opposite policy, in fact, is healthier, as is shown by some countries that, despite their own shortage of vocations, have sent several hundred missionaries to Africa alone. Long on the receiving end of missionary efforts, it is now our turn to send.

Religious Priests

Another consequence of clear thinking in regard to the role of the religious vocations relates to priests who are also religious. Lay congregations, which are made up solely of brothers, such as the Marists, the de LaSalle Brothers, and women's congregations, are not faced with this problem. They live their religious vocations as a full and unequivocal consecration without the responsibilities of the ministerial priesthood.

From early on, clerical institutes have known the subtle dichotomy between the religious and the priestly vocations when they are engaged in by one person. In general, in male religious communities throughout the world, priestly vocations predominate in organizing and formation for apostolic mission and in its exercise. Once the novitiate, or at most the initial stages of training are complete, most young male religious begin looking decisively toward the priesthood. This becomes their major goal and that choice eclipses their understanding of the religious vocation. Once ordained, young religious may have less in common with other religious than with diocesan priests. They may frequently skip meetings of their orders but seldom of their fellow priests. In essence, their primary identification tends to be with the priesthood. They come to see ministerial activities as more specific and objective than the existential challenges of a community life of spirituality and prayer.

Without realizing it, they become absorbed into the often individualistic and relatively autonomous lifestyle of the secular clergy, particularly when they are confronted with conflicts between priestly life and the implications of their vows of poverty and obedience. In the context of their vow of chastity, they are likewise prone to make common cause with secular clerics in the discussion over the eventual suppression of the celibacy requirement for priests. This is so, despite the fact that were the church's discipline on priestly celibacy to be modified, it would not apply to the religious priests. For the orders, a life of chastity and of consecrated celibacy is an integral and substantive element of their religious vocation. Still, it is evident that there is often too little awareness of this fact, and this includes many religious who are also presbyters. This is a matter for real concern.

Those of us who are involved in training candidates for religious life know how difficult it is to impress an adequate awareness of the existential priority of the religious vocation upon aspirants and novices. While there is not real incongruity between a presbyterial and a religious vocation, we need to recognize the differences between them, particularly when they are joined in one person. If we ask which of these vocations is more substantive for ordained religious, it must be stressed that the religious vocation should enjoy real, existential priority over the functional and ministerial vocation to the priesthood. It is important to reflect on and deal with the apparent fact that the opposite perception often dominates the self-understanding of priests who are consecrated to the religious life.

Adequate Formation

Adequate formation is the third and most urgent consequence for understanding clearly the role of the religious vocations. Clerical institutes must keep in mind what we have just discussed. The formation of young religious must not lead to vocational confusion or to minimizing in any degree their interrelationship and close connection when the two vocations—religious and priestly—are presented. What we are calling for here is a conscious, lucid integration of two vocations. This will contribute to an awareness, during the formative years and throughout the rest of their lives, of the two dimensions of their calling. Each makes its own demands and contributions to the apostolic fulfillment of their mission.

As we have said, this is not a problem for the lay congregations of brothers or for the women's orders. This does not mean, however, that the tension within the religious priesthood does not impinge upon their understanding and formation. Both brothers and sisters must reflect on the meaning of this tension. This will help them in two ways.

First of all, it will help brothers and sisters to develop criteria to safeguard their own religious vocations against yielding to the subtle temptation to become clerical, even as they exercise their apostolic and pastoral ministries. This clericalization can take place when they are called upon to enter ministries to make up for the deficit in numbers of secular priests for many parishes. Doing so, of course, can be a help to the people of God and a short-term solution for dioceses that are short of priests. Nevertheless, one must remain alert to the nature of the religious vocation so as not to let it be absorbed and altered by involvement in inappropriate apostolic works. More than anything else, it is one of our weaknesses that we are not always prepared to handle power *evangelically.*

Second, the faithfulness of brothers and sisters to the basics of their consecrated vocation can be of great spiritual help when they fraternize with religious priests. By the same token, their presence in projects, meetings, study sessions, and other initiatives offers opportunities for deepening and for mutual enrichment.

4

Inculturation and the Religious Vocation

The Meaning and Implication of Inculturation

Inculturation is a recently coined term with cultural-anthropological overlays that has come into common usage in theology and missiology. Catholic sensitivity toward the relationship between faith and cultures gained momentum at Vatican II and increased after the 1974 Synod on Evangelization and Paul VI's publication in 1975 of the Apostolic Exhortation *Evangelii Nuntiandi*. This discussion has enriched theological reflection as well as ecclesial-missiological praxis.

The faith and culture interface began to be called inculturation at the International Synod on Catechetics in 1977. We are not, then, dealing here with a passing theological or missiological vogue. Inculturation denotes a specific quality of an authentic evangelization process. It affirms that there can be no break between faith and culture when we evangelize. *Inculturation* should be distinguished from two other cultural processes or notions, often called acculturation and adaptation (with different nuances) by anthropologists.

Acculturation is the transformation process that comes about through contacts between a person or group and another culture. This happens in evangelization, for example, when a German missionary comes to Brazil. He or she becomes acculturated when the Brazilian Portuguese language is learned and local customs in such things as eating and dressing are adopted. When different cultural groups meet, acculturation may entail asymmetrical relations between dominant and dependent cultures. This is why the term *acculturation*, which had been used to designate what is deemed desirable in the evangelizing process, is no longer acceptable or adequate. There is always the risk of an "evangelization of culture" when one culture, in which the gospel is already present, acts upon a receptor culture, which it tries to evangelize by imposing upon it the cultural traits of the evangelizer.

Adaptation is the process of adjusting to the culture receiving the gospel—internally or externally—by the evangelizer (in manners of acting and being) and in translating and expressing the message. The ancient proverb, When in Rome do as the Romans do, is about adaptation. It is not a question of making profound changes but of relative, tactical adjustments. Adaptation can be permanent or temporary. For example, the use of drums and dance in Catholic liturgies in Africa could be a mere external adaptation lacking deeper concern for how Africans express themselves in celebrating liturgically in their own cultures. In the same way, Bible translation into the vernacular languages is no more than adaptation when it is a merely linguistic equation between two cultural traditions. A Portuguese translation of Shakespeare is an adaptation. His plays can be truly understood only in the context of his own cultural universe—an English way of thinking, acting, and imaging.

Inculturation takes place when the receptor culture takes an active part in assimilating the gospel message and translates it according to its own cultural ways of being, acting, and communicating. Through the process of inculturated evangelization the seeds of the gospel are sown in the soil of a receptor culture. The soil in which a seed falls helps determine the future of a plant; likewise, the seed of faith germinates in the cultural soil in which it is planted. Inculturation, then, is an evangelization process through which the Christian life and message are assimilated by a culture in such a way that they are not only expressed in relevant cultural terms (acculturation and adaptation) but become part of the culture itself. The gospel becomes that culture's inspiration, norm, and unifying force for transformation, recreating it and thrusting it forth.

Inculturation therefore implies and connotes a profound relationship between faith and culture deeper than a mutual adjustment of two parallel phenomena, which is basically what occurs in acculturation or adaptation. Both faith and culture relate to the totality of human life at the personal and community levels, and authentic inculturation occurs at that level.

By *Christian faith* I mean a conscious and free response—existential and experiential—by persons and communities who receive and accept God's gift of life in Jesus Christ. By *culture* I mean the complex of meanings, values, and traits implicit in the action and communication of human groups and societies, which they accept as appropriate and distinctive expressions of their own identity. Inculturation is not a discrete act but an active process that requires mutual acceptance and dialogue, critical awareness and discernment, faithfulness and conversion, transformation and growth, renewal and innovation. It is, therefore, not cultural archeology but living faith and living culture. Gospel inculturation is not a matter of looking in the past for a static cultural blueprint—in fact no longer extant—in order to plan the stages of the evangelization process. For example, if we are to inculturate the gospel in today's Afro-Brazilian culture, we cannot return to those elements that characterized African culture during the slave-trading era in the sixteenth and seventeenth centuries. That culture, which was brought here, no longer exists, either in Africa or in Brazil. To inculturate the gospel in the Afro-Brazilian culture is a process which takes as its reference point that culture's current expressions, continuing evolution, and influence upon all of Brazilian culture in which Afro-Brazilians live.

Neither is inculturation a kind of theological archeology that deals with the present in the light of a single theological point of view imported from the past. This is like trying to understand and interpret the gospel message today as it was understood in the Middle Ages, the Renaissance, the nineteenth century, or even just prior to Vatican II. Inculturation makes us aware that revelation must be announced to specific persons and groups in their own particular contexts and taking their cultural milieus into account. In the pedagogy of Yahweh in the Old Testament, of Jesus and Paul in the New, and of the church, guided by the Spirit throughout history, the process of evangelization is always concerned about education and communication. Both dimensions imply taking our dialogue partners seriously—what they inherently are, their historical context, their level of understanding and capacity to assimilate, and their forms of expression.

The evangelizer and the evangelized are both subjects of the process and should remain attentive to each other's cultural and historical contexts, as well as to the unique action of the Holy Spirit. Inculturated evangelization requires giving and receiving. There is interaction between the culture of the evangelizer and that of the evangelized. They get to know each other better and to see each other with more critical eyes. Above all, both allow themselves truly to be evangelized by the other, that is, to be guided by a gospel that is not the exclusive preserve of either one. The breach between faith and culture was a problem in the past, as Paul VI reminded us (*Evangelii Nuntiandi* 19), and continues to be so today.

If we keep in mind what we have said regarding faith and culture, inculturated evangelization is no mere transfer or modification of languages and methods, rites and symbols, organizations and norms—of external ways of action and expression. This is nothing more than acculturation and adaptation. Inculturation must go deeper, to the foundations and roots of culture (*Evangelii Nuntiandi* 19), to its values, criteria, worldviews, and ethos (i.e., the inspiration for the sociocultural praxis of a people). Inculturated evangelization plumbs the very depths of personal experience, and thus of culture and society, while it keeps in mind the complex network of relationships among peoples, God, and nature.

This is a dynamic process of conversion or reordering which is both personal and corporate.

Inculturation is processed also in terms of the ethical implications of faith. These require us to transform and perfect the structures of society. It is not the same to speak about inculturated evangelization as it is to speak of the evangelization of culture. The latter is a one-dimensional and linear exercise which takes the evangelizer's culture as an external reference point. In the past, the culture of gospel-bearing tended too often to be dominating and exclusive, imposing its own values upon cultures that were being evangelized. In contrast, the starting point of inculturated evangelization is the internal structures and meanings of host cultures, which are themselves the subject of their own evangelization. The receptors need not slavishly imitate the cultural forms in which the evangelizer communicates the gospel. Rather, they should be encouraged to rework the message from within their own cultural reality—their identity, history, values, and worldviews—in the light of gospel inspiration.

Inculturation in the Bible and in Theology

The unfolding of salvation history is a process of inculturation. God's saving project is open to all humanity in every time and place. Yet God's revelation was specifically to a particular people, Israel. They thus became the reference point for both the liberating action of God and our response to God from within our own cultural contexts. Diverse cultures made up the sociocultural fabric of the chosen people, as can be seen in both nomadic and settled phases of their history. God uses the tempering of history and the plurality of cultures that are part of the diverse situations in which Israelites found themselves throughout their history—in Mesopotamia, Egypt, Canaan, Persia, and during the post-exilic, Hellenistic, late Judaic, and Greco-Roman periods—to convey various facets of the divine-human economy. God, in effect, makes successive use of cultures without rejecting or denying values in earlier stages in Jewish history. The various cultural phases of Israel are at once continuous and discontinuous, interactive and integrative (see the Vatican II document on revelation, *Dei Verbum* 13-16). The starting point of revelation is the living reality of Israel and its evolution in understanding itself and God. God communicates with the people through persons, situations, events, and manifestations that are both contingent and relative.

Accordingly, we cannot justify viewing any culture as absolute, not even Israel, as the only and unalterable form in which divine revelation can be expressed. Still Israel remains an indispensable and decisive point of reference, precisely because it was in this people that God became inculturated through Jesus Christ. Simultaneously, we cannot *exclude* any culture from its potential to become the bearer of revelation. In fact, God loves the whole of humanity and has left in every culture and in every time signs and vestiges of the divine action in and through them. Still, no culture has the right of being a privileged vehicle of revelation. This affirmation is rooted in Christian faith and is supported by our experience of the vicissitudes of salvation history. The Word who is God, without setting aside divinity, became fully human in Jesus Christ (Jn 1:1-14; Phil 2:5-8). Through the incarnation, God has been inculturated in an original and most radical form in a specific cultural space and time. In that process we have become heirs of the theological heritage of Israel and been given insight into the prototypical example of the entire inculturation process. Founded as it is theologically and christologically upon the mystery of the incarnation, inculturation is the unique expression of mission and evangelization.

Jesus, while rooted in his own culture, kept a critical distance from it. He appropriated and affirmed the historical teleology and vocation of his own people's response to God. In other words, as a constant and irrevocable sign of the divine initiative, Jesus assumed a salvation history that was part of the history of his people. Yet Jesus also confronted and denounced, corrected and redirected what had gone astray or become perverted in the culture of the people of Israel, sidetracking or frustrating God's salvific plan. He challenged his people and his culture to conversion and transformation.

This same thing must go on permanently in the history of every culture, even if it was once evangelized. Evangelization is never fully achieved to a degree that cultures—like individuals—are dispensed from the need for continuing conversion and transformation. This is an important insight regarding the culture of evangelizers and those whom they would evangelize and in regard to inculturation. In fact, as a human reality, any culture is merely one culture among many. All have ontological, psychological, ethical, and teleological limitations. No culture should pretend to be an absolute, unique, and ideal vehicle of revelation. No culture should identify itself fully with the gospel. Nor can the gospel ever become a culture, for even though the gospel only exists when it is inculturated into a host cultural fabric, tension between gospel and culture will always exist. For this reason there is room in every culture for growth and for changing deficient attitudes. There is always a tension between faithfulness to culture in the evangelization process and a critique from culture of its openness to the gospel. The gospel must be a teacher to culture. But every culture represents a potentially new interpretation and a unique contextualization of the gospel. Evangelizers from other cultures are, together with the gospel receptors, subjects of their own evangelization.

Inculturation in Church History

The process of planting the church in its beginnings and during the first centuries of its history reveals a great openness to cultures and constant adjustment to them. Originally Semitic, the church was first planted in the Jewish Diaspora and did this as part of a far-reaching process of cultural mediation. In that process the evangelists set down in writing the content of the New Covenant in Greek narrative style. Secondly, through the early ecumenical councils, the church developed theoretical approaches to the Christian mystery, using the Greek and Latin cultural categories. In the resulting Greco-Roman synthesis, the Fathers, as well as Eastern and Western monks, took the Greek and Latin cultures for their basic models. This was the context of theology, spirituality, and pastoral action throughout the greater part of the first millennium of the Christian era, especially in the West. The greatest and perhaps most complete processes of Christian inculturation of the gospel took place in this context. In it, Christian faith was assimilated and rephrased on the basis of the elements and genius of an evangelized Greco-Roman culture, and was no longer an expression of faith in Semitic-Jewish cultural patterns, despite fundamental faithfulness to the core of the gospel.

Beginning in the third quarter of the first millennium, of course, Nordic and Slavic peoples were brought into the Christian faith. While the evangelizers were mindful of these cultures—in particular their symbolic and legal structures—and in many ways receptive toward them, the primary norms in that missionary process were rooted in Greco-Roman culture.

During the early centuries of the second millennium the church hammered together a multicultural Western European synthesis catalyzed by the events that gave rise to medieval Christianity. What resulted came to be seen as normative Catholic-Christian culture, which would be the frame of reference for evangelization during three-quarters of the second millennium. This worldview became the preferred vehicle of expressing the Christian faith and was often juridically defined as the only valid bearer of the gospel. Reaction against the Protestant Reformation in the Counter-Reformation coincided with the colonization and evangelization of new continents in the beginnings of the modern missionary movement and included the attempt to create a unified and universal Christianity characterized by the relative cultural uniformity of Western, Latin Catholicism. Thus, the models for early modern evangelization were largely forced to take place exclusively within the boundaries of one culture at the price of eclipsing, repressing, or at the very least suppressing other potential cultural expressions. *The missionary movement, in other words, in contradistinction to contemporary views of culture as an empirical reality, began with a view that saw classical Western culture as normative. With rare exceptions, this presupposition was unchallenged by the bearers of the gospel.*

To summarize, during the first centuries of the Christian era, the church moved from a theological-christological model of biblical inculturation to a christological-ecclesiological model. During the closing years of the first millennium and the major portion of the second, the historical-political model—that of a quasi-normative European-Christian cultural superiority—held sway in the West and was extended to other regions in the world. Reaction to this hegemonic model is vital if one is to understand contemporary efforts to inculturate the gospel. When this (Western) cultural model of Christian life was spread as the best—in fact, the only—vehicle for evangelization, inculturation in the ancient Israelite and early Christian senses retreated and almost disappeared from the life and witness of the church. In its place acculturation based on the normativity of Western culture was established. As a consequence, the possibility of synthesizing faith and culture was shattered. Christian faith in Western garb was dissociated from the multiplicity of cultures that began to impinge upon the new stage of world history. There were significant, though sporadic, examples of adaptation (Ricci, De Nobili, Anchieta, Nóbrega, and others), but rarely were their efforts allowed to grow to maturity in an effective non-Western inculturation of the gospel. For non-European peoples, to embrace the Christian faith would always require a surrender of indigenous culture and entail the attempt to appropriate the Western cultural package in which the gospel was delivered to them.

Religious Life and Inculturation

Consecrated religious life is a Christian and ecclesial vocation that stands out because of the public profession of its followers—as individuals and as embodied in communities. The primary life objective of religious is to live out radical implications of the gospel in both the church and the world. Consecrated religious life, as a Christian vocation, is directly linked to evangelizing mission. This mission compels us to understand the message of Jesus Christ, which by implication becomes the message of religious.

The international character of numerous religious communities, which are by definition multicultural in character, raises the issue of the connection among faith, life, and culture. For members of such congregations, this kind of connection is part and parcel of their daily being and doing, and of their apostolic praxis in evangelizing mission. Inculturation, then, must be a central topic, not only in ecclesial praxis and theological and missiological reflection, but also in the consecrated life. This is particularly the case today, because until quite recently religious institutes have been characterized by a monocultural uniformity despite their internationality. Indeed, those communities have been mostly ruled according to the cultural assumptions and practices of the areas in which they were founded. There has been relatively little space given to constructive reflection on their actual multicultural experience. At the same time, scant attention has been paid to the cultures in which these communities, lived, worked, and were planted around the world.

The Identity of Religious Institutes

The various religious institutes of the church have their own distinctive ways of examining and reading the Word and of living the gospel. These traditions are a key to understanding their respective contributions to apostolic action as they further the mission of Jesus Christ.

Religious institutes and orders generally trace their origins to a founder. The Spirit is viewed within the institute as having helped these founders—men or women—to discern, at the appointed time, a specific ecclesial need. They are believed to have been impelled to demonstrate a new aspect, or some overlooked dimension, of the gospel in the evangelical profile of the church. At the intersection of these two factors—the historical moment and an evangelical insight concerning the world and the church—founders discern something new because of their particular sensitivity to the Word and their dedication to the church. It was thus that Francis of Assisi, for example, was alerted by the Spirit to the evangelical urgency of a simple life of poverty in the midst of a church characterized by power and wealth during the time of Innocent III. During the Industrial Revolution in the nineteenth century, Dom Bosco and many other founders of orders were innovative in perceiving the importance of a potential educational mission of the church among the working classes.

A unique intuition and divine dynamism act within founders in what is commonly called a *founding charism*. Founders respond positively to the divine challenge and dedicate their lives to achieving a goal. They may not always understand clearly the nature of their inspiration to create something new. But quite often the force of their charism attracts others who share the same concerns and prepare, as an apostolic body, to serve the church and the people of God. Religious institutes, therefore, emerge within defined time-space frameworks. They are recognized, approved, and legitimated by the church in situations which can be identified with specific historical periods. *Founding charisms* are defined by the historical and sociocultural coordinates of a particular epoch in the same way that each person is born into a particular people, culture, and society. The human and spiritual character of the founders are also involved—their faith and vision, based upon particular understandings of the gospel and of God, and of their experience of God. The social and spiritual dimensions converge in a unique synthesis to constitute a person with individual characteristics, education, culture, social location, and experience.

This synthesis is significant and motivational. It can plug into an extant spiritual tradition, such as the Benedictine, Carmelite, Franciscan, Dominican, or Augustinian orders. Alternatively, new traditions are created which, nonetheless, are often indebted to earlier streams of spirituality. This was the case with such innovative men as Ignatius Loyola and Charles de Foucauld. Each order has its own emphasis and peculiar accents through which men and women understand reality and listen to the Word of God. Each unifies and provides order to the various elements of profound existential experiences. As the gift of Jesus Christ was offered to us in a specific time and culture frame, so it is with founding charisms. In sum, there is a specific connection between founding charisms and the historical moments and sociocultural contexts in which they originally appeared.

Times change, however, and the church marches through history. Religious orders expand and spread into other latitudes. The significance and survival of their charisms depend upon their rootedness in the gospel, and on the independence and flexibility of adapting to new sociocultural contexts. Religious are not only followers but living continuations of Jesus and of their founders. But they do not live in first-century Palestine, or in the fifth, thirteenth, sixteenth, eighteenth, or nineteenth centuries, the most fruitful times for religious foundations. On the contrary, in every period of history until the Parousia we must discover anew the pertinence of the gospel and of a founding charism in order to unveil its radical and authentic inspiration.

During the past five centuries, as we have seen, the church bestowed pride of place upon classical Western European culture. Virtually every diffusion of the gospel was made to pass through the same uniform ecclesiastical models. In contrast with its experience of diversity in the first millennium, evangelization during the second half of the second millennium constructed church unity on a Western and European cultural paradigm. Religious institutes, most of which originated in Southern

Europe, were useful instruments and transmitters of this uniformity because of their homogeneous rules and ways of life. Today, by contrast, there is awareness of religious as part of a world church that is engaged in a process of inculturation. This entails a different attitude and a sense of urgency about inculturation within the religious orders.

Inculturation and Charism

The inculturation of religious institutes in the evangelizing process has been discussed in conferences of superiors general and in numerous regional and continental meetings of superiors, at meetings of confederations of religious, and at national conferences of religious in various parts of the world.

In the first place, we must approach the charisms of religious and other kinds of apostolic communities in their present historical and sociocultural contexts; likewise, we must consider their present significance, as was done in the approach of Vatican II. In this vein, Pope Paul VI invited religious to undertake renewal in his Motu Proprio to religious, *Ecclesiae Sanctae*. That document led to the rewriting of the constitutions of many institutes within a process of general chapters convened to undertake renewal and updating. These efforts benefitted from historical studies on the origin and evolution of the orders. They also generated broad participation and involvement and resulted in an inevitable diversity of views on how to apply founding charisms in pastoral activity.

This process often created or revealed tensions between faithfulness to expressions of nonformal teaching and creativity in the process of exercising the charism in changed situations. Faithfulness, ideally, will depend upon the capacity to discover the evangelical source of the charism in circumstances different from those in which it was originally manifested. Creativity supposes a capacity to sense in the present *future* implications of the original charism. For example, in the eighteenth or nineteenth century, a founder may have sensed that the educational demands of gospel life could best be expressed in schools. Today, that same pedagogical dimension could guide the apostolic mission of the order in faithfulness to the charism to other forms and expressions of teaching. Today the Franciscan tradition, at a time when we are aware of structural oppression, can add to the charism of poverty a dimension of justice and liberation which the poverty that St. Francis lived in the thirteenth century was unable to discern, much less to practice.

In the second place, as I have said, inculturation will not allow us to transplant into very different cultures a single way of acting apostolically, in static faithfulness to the original charism and its sociocultural context. Instead, we must ask the following questions: How do we respond effectively to specific sociocultural and ecclesial realities while we perform apostolic service in line with our particular charism and spiritual tradition? How can we derive inspiration from the cultures in which we find ourselves to make our lifestyle more like theirs? How do we keep before us the cultural presuppositions, the meanings, values, and worldviews of receptor cultures, allowing them to shape our lifestyle and to help us restate formulas that inspired us? How do we convey all of the above during the formation process of candidates to our communities in ways that our candidates are not made to reject their own cultures in order to join our institutes?

The specific answers to these questions and the models of religious and apostolic life that ensue will necessarily be diverse. Are not the sociocultural and ecclesial realities in each continent, country, and local church different? In the midst of their diversity, however, care must be taken to preserve the appropriate note of unity that comes from the gospel and the founding charism. This will ensure that within each specific sociocultural and ecclesial context, the different apostolic contributions of each tradition can be identified.

The church and its religious orders are called to construct profound unity in the midst of diversity while respecting and valuing the richness of cultural plurality. Thus we rediscover within the religious orders the same basic theme of inculturation of the faith and unity in diversity. The gospel is independent of any culture, even while it must use culture as its medium. There is in the gospel, accordingly, a fundamental universality which can only be expressed in the particular. Starting from concrete particularity, the conditions are given for its universalization. This was the way of incarnation, as it has been throughout the history of salvation.

Analogously, we can say that concrete, specific religious charisms, when they are discerned in a process of radical evangelical inspiration, are potentially universal. While founders experienced these charisms in particular contexts, we can live them differently in numerous other cultural environments. This shows the potential universality, the actual catholicity of our founders and foundresses. To reduce these charisms to the sociohistoric coordinates of previous times and places is to deprive them precisely of the breadth of the universal gospel, which is for all time.

The dynamic tension among faithfulness, creativity, universality, and particularity will guarantee the meaningful survival of a religious order. But the confinement of a charism within the historical boundaries of its origins—in a purely material or servile faithfulness to the founder's model—is an anachronism. This would explain the eventual loss of significance with the passing of time, of which there are numerous examples both past and present.

The Importance for Mission of Inculturated Religious Life

Religious life deserves special mention in the context of the church's inculturation because of the significance and indispensable apostolic presence of religious, particularly in the so-called Third World. Because religious institutes today are closely joined to the pastoral efforts of local churches, religious life requires dynamic inculturation at the level of pastoral action, and institutional administration. Therefore the historical process of religious life is never static but characterized by continuous evolution as it meets the urgent needs of the people of God. The charismatic and prophetic dimensions of religious life, in fact, should prevail over organizational and institutional paradigms. This makes relevant the evangelical presence and international influence of religious both in the past and the present.

The future of evangelization, from the perspective of linkage of faith and culture, will depend in great measure upon whether religious understand and put into practice the principles of inculturation. This is not limited to ethnic cultures or to foreign minorities, or even to what was once called mission territories. I am referring to every type of group or human community that needs to be evangelized—parishes, lay groups and movements, base ecclesial communities, groups of young people or of married couples, and so forth. Special attention needs to be given to oppressed groups and cultures—Indians and Blacks, the poor and migrants, women, ghettos, and minorities of every kind. Every human group can be seen and treated as a specific culture or subculture, to which the definition of culture we suggested earlier applies. All such groups in every part of the world require from us the effort to make it an inculturated evangelization process. This becomes all the more urgent because of the accelerated cultural changes that are taking place in our world today under the influence of science and technology, particularly instantaneous mass communication. A large measure of the church's inculturation praxis will depend upon the inculturation praxis of the religious orders, particularly those which constitutionally are dedicated to an international apostolate.

Conclusion

In this chapter I first attempted to explain the meaning of inculturation from an anthropological and theological perspective. I then proceeded to show the analogy between inculturating the gospel and inculturating founding charisms and—by extension—religious life in its various forms. I have not tried to be overly specific with examples of this process, or to point out the means of fulfilling the task. There is much diversity in the way in which inculturation proceeds in various religious orders. Indeed, there is a wide variety of approaches being taken among international orders at this historical moment when the church and the world are entering into a new phase. New problems have arisen that require additional efforts to maintain congregational unity in the midst of a welter of local situations and sociocultural expressions.

5

A Crucial Option

Mission, Apostolate, and the Poor

The evangelical and ecclesial, prophetic and solidary preferential option for the poor is a basic experience and a central theme in Christian life. It can be no less so in consecrated religious life. So much has been written about this subject during the past twenty-five years that one could be excused for not going into it again; in addition, this option is already being exercised in many ways and places. More than a discrete topic, however, this option is a key reference point which must underpin any reflection concerning a gospel vocation to mission both for individuals as well as for communities.

The justification for this statement can be found in the Old Testament understanding and reflection on God, and in our own experience of the God that became man in Jesus Christ. The commitment of both testaments to the poor is clear manifestation of their nature, purpose, and will. Yahweh and Jesus not only emphasize their love for the poor, but they stand unequivocally on their side. Their attitude toward the poor is a live option. The option of the God of Israel and Jesus Christ for the poor is the central hermeneutical key for reading and comprehending the original and surprising character of our God. The God of the Covenant and God's Son, Jesus the Messiah and our Savior, have become accessible to us. However religious life may have evolved in our time and whatever direction it may take, this biblical intuition of God's pre-eminent love for the poor is inescapable. We cannot turn our backs upon the unfolding of the fundamental option's specific implications for our lives.

The Option and Insertion

This chapter seeks to offer a basic understanding of the meaning and implications of the fundamental option for the poor for consecrated and contextualized religious life. It is not my purpose to go into the practical details, since there is a wealth of documentation on the subject. Nor shall I focus primarily upon insertion into poor milieus, which is one of the best examples of how the religious orders are practicing their option for the poor. My reflections on insertion can be found in various places in this book, and I purposely have not dealt with it separately to avoid compartmentalization. I believe that insertion—as disposition and attitude, practice and experience—is one of the major fruits of the option for the poor. It can also be one of its best expressions, wherever there exists a heart for the poor among the poor. It should be said that insertion—geographical, contextual, sympathetic, and apostolic—is not only an expression of evangelical concern. It is also the starting point for many forms of inspiration in regard to structuring the church's presence in the world today. Insertion among the poor is an inspiring paradigm that stimulates other spiritual and symbolic forms of insertion, such as ecumenism, interreligious dialogue, the presence of the church in the world, and a model for the church's action in secular, professional, cultural, and political contexts.

Biblical and Theological Basis of the Option for the Poor

In the History of Israel

In Exodus, the God of Israel is revealed as savior and liberator of a poor and enslaved people. By themselves these people cannot escape their onerous condition. Because they are poor, enslaved, and powerless, they are an oppressed people. They have been robbed of their right to be that which is essential to life—their capacity to rely on themselves. They are, therefore, a people that lacks justice, which is that response to the fundamental human right to life and freedom of expression in every sense of the word. We find in Exodus a clear connection between poverty and injustice. There is such a thing as poverty that is not merely an isolated social phenomenon but the result of the active will of some over others, the result of a particular way of organizing society.

So vigorous and surprising is the experience of liberation from oppression that the Exodus of Israel becomes the basic frame of reference in its awareness of being now a free people, the source of national identity. The people of Israel define their faith in terms of their relationship to the God who liberated them. Prodded by Moses, the divine name is revealed, with all that this implies for Israel. The full liberation that took place in the Exodus becomes the central theme of their faith. Through the Exodus experience they discover the meaning of a relationship with God. Through it, what the people have awaited over successive generations becomes fact—the fulfillment of the promise to and through Abraham. That is why at every Passover feast this liberation is ritually commemorated, thus becoming part of the religious and cultural memory of the people (Ex 3:7-10; Jos 24:2-28).

The Exodus is a faith event pregnant with political implications. It is an affirmation of the kind of relationship of the people with their God. But it also defines the way in which human beings should relate to one another in society.

The basic orientation of the Covenant is revealed through the constant fulfillment of liberation from poverty and oppression. To liberate is to provide the conditions for the recovery of the human freedom which has somehow been diminished, above all, because of repression, manipulation, and oppression. To liberate is, therefore, to restore and construct justice. To liberate is to save and rescue persons in the singular, as well as entire peoples. To liberate is to transform and provide new direction for the worldviews that organize the lives of persons and groups.

Liberation through justice was the program that Yahweh gave to the judges, kings, and also to the people directly. It is the divine program in the Covenant, about which the prophets constantly reminded the people (see, for example, Is 3:14-15; Jer 22:3-13, 16,17). Freedom through justice runs through the entire history of the people of God.

In the Evangelical Perspective of Jesus

Jesus radicalized the Old Testament perspective, making it more encompassing in his own life and in the lives of those whom he calls to follow him. He evaluated the authenticity of the relationship between persons and God in the light of their relationship to other human beings (Is 61:1,2; Lk 4:16-21; 6:20-26; 10:25-37; Mt 25:31-46).

The criterion for evaluating this relationship is the kind of justice that liberates the oppressed, poor, marginalized, and those discriminated against by society and culture, by power structures and religion. Justice in their favor reestablished at every level makes their true liberation possible. In the New Testament we find again the profound connection between poverty as oppression and justice as liberation. Not only is the central evidence and original identity of the gospel paradigm made clear, but its theology, its end purpose, as well. Both identity and teleology are characterized by the way in which we, as human beings, relate among ourselves and with the God of Jesus Christ, who is also our God. The gospel, then, points us to a faith which is relational and also to a qualified relationship between us and God. That is, our relationship with God becomes possible through our relationship to others. The foundation and support for all of this is our attention to the poor, as the parable of the Good Samaritan (Lk 10:29-37) and the eschatological sermon (Mt 25:31-46) make very clear.

Jesus defined his life and mission in terms of this attention to the poor and the requirements of justice on their behalf. It is what he said in his address in the synagogue at Nazareth (Lk 4:16-21)—inspired by the prophet Isaiah (61:1,2)—that the Isaian promise was being fulfilled in him before the eyes of his listeners. This scene is repeated when the Baptist sends his disciples to ask him if he is the one who is to come or if he should wait for another (Lk 7:18-23). Jesus does not answer straightforwardly that he is the Messiah. However, underlining the continuity between prophecy and its fulfillment, he makes his identity clear by citing the same text in Isaiah 61:1,2: "The Spirit of the Lord Yahweh has been given to me, for Yahweh has anointed me. He has sent me to bring good news to the poor, to bind up hearts that are broken; to proclaim liberty to captives, freedom to those in prison; to proclaim a year of favor from Yahweh, a day of vengeance for our God." This is how we can recognize him.

Motivated by this basic inspiration, Jesus appears as a man for others, a person for whom the others are primarily the sick and deprived, publicans and sinners, strangers, women, and children. These are precisely the poor of his time—the ones that society and culture, civil and religious power, marginalize and discriminate against, oppress and exclude. They are therefore those for whom liberating justice has not worked. And they are the people that in their present condition are not capable of liberating themselves.

Jesus gave these excluded ones the better part of his care and time. To them he devoted his energies, words, presence, and power to change. This dynamic of transformation, which is so present in the gospel, is what allows us to speak about an "option"; that is, a coherent and operative decision by Jesus that was based on certain ideals to which he was totally committed. Jesus made clear, through the positions that he took and the challenges that he posed, his opposition to many aspects of the society in which he lived and with aspects of the religion in which he was brought up. He does not hesitate to get to the very nerve of the relationship with God and neighbor. From this follows the hierarchy of commandments. By placing the poor neighbor first, without excluding the non-poor, with whom he also had dealings, Jesus makes it clear—through his life more than through his words—that simple folk and little people are his priority option. It cannot be said that Jesus' option was for the wise and educated, the scribes and Pharisees, the powerful of every kind. But we can state with certainty, because it is easy to demonstrate, that he opted preferentially for the poor of his time.

This internal and external liberation produces LIFE. Jesus defined himself as "life" (Jn 14:8). He is the one who brings life and does so abundantly (Jn 10:10). His life and the life that he restores in people are expressions in themselves of the presence of the Kingdom, which is itself life. Jesus announced this, in a particular historical context, in terms of building and practicing justice. He taught that this was the unmistakable and definitive direction that life must take.

Because of this fundamental inspiration in his life and work, Jesus broke with many religious paradigms that provided meaning and legitimization to oppressive societies. Such paradigms are characterized by what is given and received, imposed and prescribed, untouchable and immutable, that is to say, by everything stratified, discriminatory, and oppressive.

Jesus established the equality of all before God, an equality that is the source of every impulse toward justice. He did not reject diversity, but respected it and incorporated it into his praxis. He did, however, reject any assumption that diversity justifies inequality. By this same token, basic equality firmly requires solidarity with everyone, particularly with those whom sociocultural and politico-religious organizations have marginalized or excluded.

Jesus thus used a theological standard to transform the anthropological nature and quality of interpersonal and social relations. By making this quality the very criterion for true relationships between human beings and God, Jesus reinforced the prophetic insight into this as foundation for the radical transformation of the social fabric, including religious life and activity. He opened up the possibility of a new human community to be founded on liberating justice. It would be built upon the truth of love in solidarity, which is the basis of communion and makes community possible.

It is our task to build this new human community in the world. God makes us part of this stream of redemption, which is liberation in and through Jesus. Because of it, the God of Jesus Christ is manifested in and through us to make God's presence known in the world. If this dimension is missing, our faith is sterile and aberrant. Even while we might cultivate an intimate relationship with God, that kind of faith could never be Christian, because the ethical means to challenge and transform it would be missing. Because it is incarnational and historical, the Christian faith can never do without this ethical imperative. The option for the poor, in the terms espoused, is both an ethical means and a sign of theological faith.

The Poor among Us

The situation of grinding poverty and oppression in the world today, particularly in the southern hemisphere, sometimes called the Third

World, but also in huge pockets of poverty in both the First World and in the immense dislocation and unrest we see today in the Second World (the former socialist countries), makes the connection between poverty and oppression all the more evident. Those who suffer will hardly escape from this kind of poverty, which is increasingly generated and invigorated by the dynamics of local and international social structures. In ways similar to the Old and New Testament worlds, what we find in daily life throughout our world today is oppressive poverty. This is the result of injustice that is not circumstantial but institutional. It is part of the long-term consolidation of a de facto hegemonic legislation of a powerful market praxis. This flagrant form of institutionalized economic violence has become normative in society. What we have here is not merely a circumstantial or incidental poverty. Rather, it is a structural poverty that is part and parcel of our world's social fabric.

The poor of this world have become, then, what may be termed a *sacrament* revealing the need for a new Exodus, a new liberation, the fulfillment of which is within our grasp to effect and therefore our responsibility. It is one of the signs that can revive in us the mission of Jesus Christ. He wants to link us to himself in this aspect of his mission. But this will not become reality in us until the ethical implications of our faith have been translated into reality.

When it became aware of the real situation, when it had perceived, analyzed, and interpreted the radical dimensions of this poverty in the light of the Word of the Lord, the Latin American church took a momentous step. It declared its option for the poor, calling it *evangelical and ecclesial, prophetic and solidary, preferential and a priority* at Medellín in 1968, at Puebla in 1979, and at Santo Domingo in 1992. Other churches have echoed this sensitivity—the Canadian and French bishops in their pastoral letters of 1982, and the U.S. bishops in their great 1986 document about the economy of the United States and the world.

This option became a pertinent instrument, a major means for transforming the world and the church in the world. It is an *epistemological* and sociological, theological and ecclesial means that brings together faith and life, word and deed, apostolic mission and pastoral praxis. The option for the poor points the way to profound and urgent changes required in global sociocultural, economic, and political structures.

The Semantics of the Option for the Poor

The option for the poor, as a specific lifestyle, is often misunderstood or rejected. The concept needs to be clearly defined. On a broad semantic scale, overgeneralization, on the one hand, has emptied it of its true meaning, and on the other, intransigent positions have resulted in exaggerated polarization.

These two extreme positions, both of them ideological, practically cancel out the true meaning and implications of the option for the poor. The first feels uncomfortable with the challenge. It attempts to rationalize and transfer the question of poverty to the realms of the circumstantial, sociological, and spiritual. Insisting upon poverty of spirit, this interpretation assures us, reading scripture one-sidedly, that the poor shall always be with us. Poverty, it says, is a social and sociological problem that we can count on. This attitude leaves no room for a commitment to transformation, and shows even less willingness to become disestablished. When this occurs, "preferential love" is substituted for the "preferential option." The language is similar, but the praxis, the lifestyle, is profoundly different.

The second position is reductionist in its interpretation of the option for the poor. It demands from everyone the same level of commitment to a specific and exclusive approach. It is to live with and as the poor, being directly involved in their everyday lives. It is to participate in their struggles, usually with a political and trade-union agenda. This would be the only convincing way of clearly translating the option in evangelical and ecclesial terms. This way of working out the option for the poor—to live in a *favela* or shanty-town, for example—becomes an ideological premise that the entire church must adopt in order to put into practice the option for the poor, personally and communally.

As happens with all extremes, both positions are caricatures. In practice they cannot be found in their purest form. So it may be helpful to consider, in some depth, the meaning and significance of the option for the poor.

What the Option for the Poor Is Not

The option for the poor does not absolutize poverty or glorify the poor, as if poverty were desirable and therefore should remain. The poor are not, because they are poor, the perfect expression of the Christian message. Nor are they exempt from human limitations and sins.

The option is not a naive pretense that the poor cannot aspire to social mobility to overcome their situation, certainly not the subhuman wretchedness that can be found in the Third World and also in parts of the First World.

It does not entail patronizing the poor, manipulating their plight to serve the interests of some or to help others gain party votes.

The option for the poor is not a mechanism for bringing together and organizing the poor to gain political power or to increase trade-union membership.

What the Option for the Poor Really Is

It is an *existential* option which emerges from the very depths of our being. It is demonstrated through poverty of spirit, by a solicitous and respectful concern for others, and by the capacity to be open to others without imposing ourselves on them. It is, therefore, contrary to self-sufficient pride, which has an answer for everything and that attempts to impose itself upon everyone. The preferential option occurs in those who are open to it—whether before or after they practice it. In a continuous feedback, the option can move us toward the poor or the poor can impel us toward it. We go out to evangelize the poor and they end up evangelizing us, to quote an infinitely wise aphorism.

The option is, therefore, a radically *evangelical* option that qualifies our Christian identity. It is openness to the work of the Spirit that impels us to appropriate the values and criteria, the attitudes and preferences of our Lord Jesus. It must then be the option of every Christian, even while it will work out in many different ways. However, in every case two questions must be asked: Do the same feelings as Jesus had toward the poor of his time live in me concerning the poor around me? Do these sentiments motivate me to build a new and just society in the light of the understanding that we have today of the structural production of poverty in such a large scale throughout the entire world?

This option is a priority, but not exclusively (see Puebla documents, paragraph 1134) for those that Jesus himself favored. They are not the wise, rich, and powerful, but the little ones, simple folk, the poor and marginalized. In his option for the poor, Jesus did not follow the way of the power factions of his day—Herodians or Romans, Zealots or Essenes, Pharisees or Sadducees, scribes, levites or priests. Nonetheless, he made an unmeasurable political impact for change upon his society and upon countless others down through history.

It is an *epistemological* option—a new way of seeing things, a new social perspective. Through the eyes of the poor we begin to see and perceive, analyze and interpret the reality in which we live. There is a historical parallel for this. Until recently, history was written about the great ones of the world: kings, priests, and warriors. More recently, a new kind of history starts with the daily lives of ordinary people and takes into account changes that are taking place in and because of them. The social location of the poor is not, therefore, merely a social category. It regards not where people are on a scale of wealth or power in a society that is made up of the rich and educated, professional, and working class, but is, instead, an epistemological category. It is a way of seeing and knowing which is available to anyone. But those who discover among the poor the evangelical meaning of poverty are better equipped to assimilate this option, because they are open to its implications, including to their own transformation. A businessman can call the unemployed lazy. But when he begins to see through the eyes of the poor, this same businessman can become aware, first of all, that unemployed persons do not have the same qualifications as he does, the same family opportunities and training. Second, this businessman can begin to perceive the pressure of circumstances, the economic and structural mechanisms that produce unemployment. He can see the poor as victims who cannot change their situation no matter how much they try. Here are two different readings of the same phenomenon—unemployment.

The option for the poor is also *theological*. It is a new way of reading the sources of our faith formation: the Bible and Tradition. This different approach takes place in the light of the evidence and relevance of the poor in the history of salvation. It is guided also by our perception of the overwhelming presence of the poor in the world, and by our concern for them. I am talking about a new theological outlook and a new theological location.

The option is also an *ecclesial* option because it redirects the church in relation to its institutional and historical past. During the greater part of this history, the church has been rich and powerful; it discriminated and oppressed. For this we have asked forgiveness from men and women of the past and present. This should allow for a new formulation of ecclesial, apostolic, and pastoral evangelization.

It is an option in *solidarity*. Because this is significant and important to us, it forces us to take responsibility for the same struggles, challenges, and commitments of the poor in order to build a just world. It is thus an option which leads us to experience the reality of the poor and, eventually, even to take part in it, whether temporarily or on a permanent basis. Many Christians of diverse vocations have carried this option to the point of death and martyrdom. Some have been priests and religious and are, in general, known and reverenced. The majority, however, are anonymous martyrs. They are committed laity who gave up their lives in the midst of their daily routines or were the victims of violent acts that were buried in the news and went unpunished.

The option is a *prophetic* option because it reminds the world and the church of the basic inspiration for the Kingdom project. Thus did the prophets remind kings and people in Israel of the terms of the Covenant and of Yahweh's liberating deeds in the Exodus. It is no less prophetic when it questions, denounces, and confronts the many faces of injustice, while it points to a new society that is egalitarian and fraternal, just and authentic, supportive and communitarian.

It is a *humane* evangelical option. It aims at a new synthesis of communion, involvement, fellowship, unity and solidarity, love and truth, where justice and peace can be constructed in freedom. The gospel then becomes specific in the integral liberation of human beings at every level—both of persons and communities, individuals and societies.

The option for the poor binds the fundamental ingredient of liberation to inculturation. This linkage occurs to the degree in which an integral process of evangelization becomes an experience of liberation and inculturation because of change in theological and sociological understandings. This process begins from within the culture of the poor and with its own presuppositions (inculturation) and moves on to actions that transform the personal and social relations among ourselves and with God (liberation).

This option is a *process* which helps us realize that the poor are active agents in their own and the church's evangelization. The church discovers how evangelical the poor are—those whom Christ declared to be the most open to the invitation of the Kingdom. The church, that is ourselves, has much to learn—and not only to teach—when it opens itself up and makes itself available to the simple folk and little people. They are becoming the subjects of their own liberation and of the world's transformation. They are not asking for magic or for extreme recipes. They do not want palliatives or philanthropic and paternalistic solutions. What the poor need is profound changes in the basic assumptions of stratified social organization, which is exclusive, centralized, and oppressive. The poor have the most to gain from a social order that is built upon freedom and justice, which they do not now have, so they can be subjects of their own history, protagonists of their own growth. They should not be kept merely as passive receptors of official and public or benevolent and private initiatives on their behalf.

I am talking, then, about an option that offers new dimensions to the personal life of every Christian and of the faith community which is the church. It speaks to us of conversion that brings us out of our self-centeredness as we respond to the most needy. We announce to them the gift of the gospel, Jesus, who is also the gospel giver. And, as we do this, we are allowing ourselves to be surprised and challenged by the very ones that we are attempting to evangelize.

Eventually, the option for the poor is *revolutionary*. When it is effectively implemented at every level—individual and social, communitarian and ecclesial—it challenges all the presuppositions that underpin the present social model, subverting them totally and completely, to their very roots. This option also implies a complete transformation in the way we reflect on faith (theology); in how we translate faith into a praxis which is evangelical and apostolic, evangelizing and pastoral. It is rooted, that is to say, in the Christian faith and its ethical implications.

Fulfilling the Option

To understand the option for the poor in these terms and to describe its broad spectrum of qualifications does not, however, guarantee that we are capable of applying it to our own lives and of translating it into apostolic service to our brothers and sisters. To achieve these goals we must let ourselves be carried by the power of the Holy Spirit in us. We must discover that the first poor for whom we have to opt are ourselves. It is we who shall be pedagogically transformed by the example and inspiration of others. We must learn from associates who are more generous and gracious than we are, who are closer to the poor and more consistent in their option.

The main consequence of this will be to multiply the ways in which the option for the poor can become specific. We are not all called to do the same thing. Talents and vocations are diverse; charisms and roles are as different and varied as ministries and functions. The important thing is that all of us, in our own way, have been called to translate this evangelical priority. For some this will mean standing with the poor, in physical unity with them. Others will work toward changing the basic laws on which the social transformations actually depend. Still others will have the ability to convey lucidly the centrality of this option through their lives, writings, work, and witness. Still others will have the grace to comprehend that sickness, age, and disabling infirmities—barriers to influence and to self-affirmation—are a form of poverty which, in another key, can tune into the plight of the poor. Whatever the situation, the intuition that we gain from an evangelical understanding of poverty is indispensable to the Christian life. The poor themselves—those who are materially, spiritually, and psychologically poor—must discover through the action of the Holy Spirit the evangelical meaning of their poverty. Otherwise they will adopt the attitudes of the rich and powerful by becoming exclusive and oppressive. This is a reason why poverty in and of itself should not be singled out as an absolute. Only the poverty that is experienced in an evangelical way is truly sacramental. Therefore, one of the missions of those who live and practice the option for the poor is to help the poor to live their poverty in an evangelical way. Such poverty can help to make them open to others, to enter into solidarity with their fellow poor, and to be able to share with them. But none of this is granted to us automatically. It is definitely a gift of grace—part of our training into the full meaning of our faith.

Who Are the Poor in the Option for the Poor?

The Poor in the Time of Jesus

The poor were those who had their freedom infringed upon, at the expense of their humanity. One is impressed to discover that everything that Jesus did for his contemporaries can be summarized in two aspects of the same gospel. First, he helped them know and love God as a Father by living as sons and daughters, in fellowship with God. But Jesus also showed them that this is not possible in a world in which human beings cannot be truly human. From the perspective of Jesus, we relate to God to the degree in which we are able to relate to each other. This presupposes a relationship in line with our Lord's purpose in creating us out of love and rescuing us through the saving power of the Son, our brother Jesus Christ. The divine plan contains a loving design for the human goal of which we are a part.

In his extensive healing ministry, Jesus opted for the poor who were psychologically and physically less free—those possessed by demons, the blind, the crippled, the deaf and the dumb, the sick of every kind. He opened the eyes of their minds and hearts so that they could sense their relationship to God with the kind of faith that Jesus always called for in his healings. He loosened their tongues to testify to the Lord. As with the man at Bethesda, he helped them walk forward in life, turning their backs upon the paralysis of their past.

The words of Jesus retrieved the meaning of human freedom before God. The parables of mercy and of the prodigal son, in particular, reveal to us Jesus' God as compassionate Father, full of mercy, and always ready to receive us. He gave us a different understanding of sin, one which emphasized our freedom and responsibility. It is a fruit which love and truth have impregnated in us. The entire Sermon on the Mount removes sin from the realm of external transgression against laws to the deeper level of intentions that affect and perturb the love relationship among human beings and between them and God. He thus freed us from fatalism and fear, from formalism and hypocritical legalism. He banished from our imaginations a mean and inhuman deity, an inflexible and miserly god. And he introduced us to a God who builds justice in love, making this our great project for the benefit of the persons whom God created. With threads of divine forgiveness and of human response, Jesus shows that God has woven us into a new creation. This creation is founded upon a restoration of freedom as shown by Magdalene, the prodigal son, and Peter and Zacchaeus.

In essence, Jesus opted for the poor whose freedom was threatened by the distortions and contradictions of their own society, culture, and religion. These aberrations were separating them from God's original plan and destroying them. Thus he rescued the poor in the Jewish world of his time: women and children, publicans and lepers, people who lived simple lives day by day, despised because they did not have access to the Law, excluded because they were absolutely powerless to make decisions.

The Poor in Our Time

The poor of Jesus' time still abound in our fields and cities. And it is still the poor for whom we must opt today. But our present world presents myriad other kinds—more complex and subtle—of poverty that distort and destroy human freedom. Today there are the landless, the jobless, and the homeless migrants; there are people everywhere who are being discriminated against. The poor among us are the illiterate who have no chance to better their education, the famished in a world that is overflowing with food. They are the indigent and sickly who languish on the doorsteps of our hospitals. The poor are those who suffer violence and pressure of every kind. They are frustrated and manipulated by political and religious power, and by the mass media.

Above all, this world of dominating economics determines that the poor are wretched, barely able to exist, living at human survival limits. They are mostly famished and discarded in a world of high technology and complexity. The group for which we must primarily opt comprises the victims of structured economic poverty. Without the basics for survival, these human beings lack the most elementary conditions for freedom. The image of God is being disfigured in them by the free acts of others, that is, ourselves. Yet paradoxically, it is in these disfigured faces that we discover the face of God that most challenges us and invites us to freely choose to engage in the urgent transformation of this universe. Our world has everything in it to meet adequately the needs of humanity and to help it fully find its way once more, as well as God's way.

Every one of the poor that I have named, in one way or the other, lacks freedom. Many, however—the deaf and dumb, for example—can live with their deficiencies and limitations. But the structural and economic poverty that comes from perverse organization debases and gradually destroys the very foundations of human freedom. Most flagrant of all is the paradox of overwhelming poverty in an affluent and rich world. We are called to opt first for these poor, without by this excluding anyone else. And this option must include an all-encompassing challenge to the society that is creating such poverty.

The option for the poor—evangelical, ecclesial, and preferential, a prophetic priority in solidarity with them—is in our world today another full expression of the evangelical project. It is a challenging substantiation of the faith we have attained through Jesus Christ. In the religious life, this is a primary means of publicly affirming our consecration to the church's responsible and effective mission in the world.

Part 2

CONSECRATION AND MISSION

Creative Faithfulness

6

Transformation Dynamics
in Religious Vocations

A Historical Retrospective on Change
in Contemporary Religious Life

Vatican Council II, primarily through *Lumen Gentium* and *Perfectae Caritatis*, established decisive elements for the direction and nature of transformations in consecrated religious life during the past twenty-five years. The Motu Proprio *Ecclesiae Sanctae* of Paul VI introduced the transformation process to religious institutes. He invited them to undertake a historical study of their origins and evolution in order to understand and interpret the fundamental insights and identities of their founders, their charisms and respective legacies. He called upon the orders to become aware of the reality of today's world and of the church in the world. Paul VI was challenging the men and women religious of the *active apostolic life* throughout the world to respond in relevant and specific ways to the demands of mission and its evangelical priorities.

There was a broad response to *Ecclesiae Sanctae* by the various institutes. The requisite historical and theological research was done, as were sociological studies into the internal situation of the congregations and the church, as well as the multiplicity of external realities within the various sociocultural, economic, and political contexts in which the orders carry out their apostolate.

Between 1967 and 1985 the general chapters of renewal gathered to classify and systematize the vast amount of material that communities from the respective orders had put together. This became the basis for rewriting—generally with great care within a participative process—new constitutions for the various orders. Apostolic projects for transforming the orders internally were also developed, as well as guidelines concerning their presence and an apostolic-ecclesial agenda for the immediate future.

The results of this process are taken into account in this chapter, which focuses particularly upon what—overall—ensued within the consecrated religious life during the twenty-five years following Vatican II. More specifically I am interested in ascertaining how the changes that took place in the decade of 1975 to 1985 were consolidated. This brings us down to our own time in the mid-nineties. We are illuminated by perceiving and comprehending the changes that have taken place in the religious life, many of them unexpected.

The consecrated religious life is one of the forms of Christian life that historically has most resisted disruptions and thorough modifications. In spite of formal differences between the orders—in particular during the millennium that we are about to conclude—there has been a fundamental continuity that remains untouched. During most of the five centuries in which we have witnessed the irruption of modernity and its complex culture, religious life remained practically unaffected, despite the radical transformations that were taking place in every sphere of human life.

After Vatican II, however, religious life in general, and segments of the women's orders in particular, were among the aspects of Christian life and vocation that registered the most profound changes in concept and focus, in expression and in operation. It is important today that superiors and formation personnel, as well as the younger generation, keep this in mind. It is especially crucial that they understand this evolution as part of a dynamic transformational process. Superiors and formation personnel, as links between past and present, must avoid the temptation both to try to bring back the past and to block the present and future. Equally important, the new generation of religious needs to understand clearly and critically their history, because it is on this history that they must build the future.

Today we find two tendencies in the religious life. On the one hand, there is a kind of restorationist fundamentalism that hangs on to past certainties and tacitly or explicitly rejects any kind of change or evolution. On the other hand is a purely prospective approach; it launches itself into the future with scant historical awareness, heedless and seemingly unconcerned that priceless treasures from the lives of previous generations are being lost and destroyed.

In the following section I shall point out the changes that are taking place in the religious life, noting specific transitions from one paradigm to another. To do so, I shall use the method of *correlation* rather than that of *comparison*. This may help us better grasp and pinpoint the nature of changes by relating the previous and present state of the religious life. As the context will make clear, I am looking for emphases and perceptible characteristics. This is not a simple catalogue of straightforward substitutions of pre–Vatican II situations with corresponding conditions after the Council. It is not unusual to find both dimensions in our congregations. There may even be a few isolated cases where the pre–Vatican II perspective still prevails. But overall, we have moved, in fact, from stressing pre–Vatican II issues to their corresponding post-conciliar emphasis.

In the present context of the church and the world, and for the fore-seeable future, the situation in the consecrated religious life can be ba-sically, though not exhaustively, characterized by the facts and features that I shall now present.

Changes in Self-Understanding and Foundation

There was, first, a transition from a preponderantly devotional and functional emphasis toward a theological foundation. The religious life, to be sure, had theological foundations from the beginning. Still, theological awareness was not central to the religious life, nor was it crucial to its subsistence and evolution. Instead, developing the devo-tional life of the members—a significant factor in the genesis of the orders—and keeping the operation functioning smoothly were the ma-jor accents for centuries. The issue of theological foundations and ratio-nale came to the fore after Vatican II. It then became necessary to legiti-mize the religious life and to make it intelligible to both present and future practitioners in a secular world that remains critical, eclectic, and pluralistic vis-à-vis religion. Establishing clear-cut theological founda-tions and rationales became central at every stage of religious forma-tion. But it is important to stress that, on the eve of Vatican II, such theological foundations were not explicitly relevant; they were, in fact, absent from many training programs, and from the minds of many of the formation directors. I speak out of the experience of my own forma-tion and from extensive data that I was able to compile during my ten-ure as chairman of the National Conference of Religious in Brazil dur-ing the significant years between 1968 and 1977. I had access to the constitutional and chapter documents from almost three hundred reli-gious communities.

Second, there was the shift from moralism and imitation to charis-matic and prophetic inspiration. The transition was from habits and vir-tues to be acquired through the imitation of ethical models to biblical-christological inspiration and an open-ended following of Jesus. Imitation of the historical Jesus (*imitatio Christi*) or of the saints (the founders of orders and others) had heavily influenced the uniform un-derstanding of how the religious life should be lived everywhere. This kind of universality was possible because of the immobility and perma-nence of the frame of reference. Internally, there was, for example, a static vision of the saints. Externally, cultural matrices dating to the years in which congregations were founded were imposed—with no perception of the need to inculturate the congregations's mission in diverse cultures. The belief that religiosity was independent of time and space allowed history to repeat itself and life to carry on without a sense of history. In contrast, the post-conciliar awareness that gospel life is not based on isolated Bible texts, but is a radical, existential response to the totality of the gospel caused the religious life to rediscover the inexhaustible potential of its charisms and the unexpected character of its prophetic vocation.

Charisms, it came to be seen, will survive to the degree in which they can be transplanted from their original sociocultural milieu into present contexts without being cut off from their roots. This is how charisms become meaningful and significant in new and different historical contexts. When charisms express a unique evangelical intuition point to a particular need within the church, the religious vocation puts into practice its prophetic role. The prophetic dimension is, for the people of God and for the church, a healthy reminder of God's original purposes. The charismatic-prophetic linkage makes the presence of Jesus real, not by a material imitation of what he was in his time, but by specific translations into what he would be today if he lived among us. This is a dynamic form of discipleship. Religious are not only imitators, nor even followers of Jesus and of the founders of their orders. They are also *continuations*, that is, persons who—having been touched by the same gift (charism)—infuse it with new life, translating it into their present context (prophecy), in the light of our fundamental reference, Jesus our Lord.

Third, there was a shift from a limited and reductionist comprehension of charism to a multiplicity of new expressions. This means a transition from a view and practice of charisms that only convey the social and cultural reality of the founders to one envisaging making them concrete in acceptable and valid forms in the various contexts of our present world. In other words, the religious orders—ideally—have moved from an institutionally rigid, formal understanding of their foundational documents, mediations, and actions to embrace a different perception of themselves. They first resurrected writings and documents that illuminated their foundations and documents within their original contexts. They exegeted them according to their literary genre and—only then—interpreted, evaluated, and properly updated the documents. At a second stage, they introduced more flexible institutional expressions beyond their original concrete forms. For example, a passage on education (which restricted members to work in schools) could have been broadened to encompass formal and informal training, popular education, and education for minorities in response to present-day pedagogical concepts, methods, and means.

Fourth, the previous approaches were made possible because of a transition from a religious life divorced from time and history to an awareness that major social changes are conditioning and distorting the religious life and its apostolic mission. This presupposes a transition from a self-defensive religious life, apart from the world and primarily concerned with safeguarding its identity, to a religious life that is critically open to the world, constructively present in it, and capable of bringing together faithfulness and creativity, continuity and discontinuity, without damaging or losing its identity.

Fifth, Vatican Council II signified the passage from a religious life that was turned in upon itself, primarily or exclusively concerned with individual perfection and salvation, to a religious life that was aware of the priority of mission and of the singular importance of community. It moved *from* cultivating order and stability and prioritizing solitude and restraint *to* internal and external community, individually or in groups. In other words, there was a transition from a centripetal understanding of religious vocation—as a privileged and more perfect response to the call to holiness—to a vision of the religious life as one among many valid church vocations. These new perceptions, in their several ways, aim at building the Kingdom by following Jesus in continuation of his mission.

Changes in the Structures of the Religious Life

During and after Vatican II a transition took place. We moved, first of all, from a view of the feminine that was male-dominated in regard to women's religious vocations, self-awareness, perspective, and femininity that suppressed and deformed. We moved to a view of the feminine that affirmed, valued, and expressed itself in several ways:

- in respect and appreciation for the self-identity of women, and their proper space and autonomy in making choices, decisions, and judgments;
- as the bearer of a vision and a subsidiary contribution to better understanding the universe in all its aspects, a universe too long apprehended and interpreted hegemonically by males;
- as a new key, discovered and rediscovered, for understanding and apprehending the God revealed in Jesus Christ, who until recently had been interpreted and expressed in purely male terms;
- as an indispensable factor for understanding rightly and more completely the total mystery of Jesus Christ—particularly for grasping the implications of his incarnation and the institutional expression of his mystical and ecclesial reality;
- as a source of creativity in the human tradition of mission through apostolic presence and action in which the totality of humanity as

male and female is expressed in an equality of conditions and diversity of ways.

Second, there is the passage from an overly individualistic, legalistic, and administrative understanding of the vows of poverty to a simpler and more austere personal and community lifestyle in solidarity with the poor. The previous lifestyle of religious, while extolling personal austerity, accumulated wealth and courted the rich. The new way of life shows a greater willingness to share, both internally and externally and in more effective ways, because it is motivated by the reality of the poor.

Third, there is the passage from seeing world poverty as an unavoidable social phenomenon to engagement in building a just social order inspired by the gospel. Whereas poverty was a fact that one had to live with—resignedly and in safety, and with charitable concern—there is today in the religious orders a new dynamic of human promotion and of social transformation.

Fourth, there is the transition from a restricted and paternalistic comprehension of world poverty from a developmentalist perspective to a growing awareness of the mechanisms of injustice that marginalize persons and groups. The mechanisms that subsume world structures and make them more interdependent and yet skewed in favor of the rich dramatize the tensions between North and South and within large pockets of urban poverty in the entire world. Religious orders are putting their awareness into practice at different levels of commitment. They are exemplifying an evangelical and prophetic, solidary and preferential option for the poor—those who lack the essentials for a decent, free, and worthy life.

Fifth, there is the passage from a life self-protectively turned in upon itself to a life of insertion in the most needy and depressed geographical and social areas. By their insertion, male and female religious are attempting to share in the life of the poor. They are trying to become part of the same causes for which the poor are struggling. They are learning to give of themselves even as they become open to receive others. It is a relationship of mutual evangelization, the aim of which is a real evangelical transformation of situations and of people. When this process is taken seriously and given a certain continuity, it becomes a source of surprising transformation for consecrated religious persons.

Sixth, we have moved from a concept of the vow of chastity which emphasizes the moral purity of individuals as the virtue of renunciation, mortification, and temperance, or as a functional means for the apostolate, toward understanding chastity and consecrated celibacy as an expression of affection fulfilled, personally and in community, offered in love to God and neighbor. Consecrated chastity thus becomes a sign of the hope of the Kingdom, an anticipation of the authentic fulfillment of the end times, and a definitive expression of human love.

Seventh, we have moved from a vow of chastity experienced as deprivation of the gifts of full sexuality, of paternity and maternity, of personal intimacy, and the physical enjoyment of love, to a view of chastity as an offering that affirms integral affection as a mature expression of freedom, and the capacity to give oneself totally and without expecting anything in return. When we fully assume these vows, they become a means of experiencing dynamically the grace of God toward us. Here we have a concrete way of demonstrating and of strengthening a genuine and selfless love that is neither possessive nor based upon selfish gratification.

Eighth, there is a transition from a view of the vow of obedience as renunciation of personal freedom and unilateral submission to the will of a superior, which was the only expression of the will of God, to a concept of obedience that is intimately tied to mission and structured by it. This leads to the perception that everyone is in obedience, those who serve in authority and the rest. They are all in obedience because everyone is responsible for some part of discernment that can help them to identify the will of the Lord for persons and groups, communities, and orders. From this follows that specific awareness of each religious person's human condition, as well as his or her history and development, that should be a primary concern in discerning the will of God. This awareness is an important factor in determining the kind and quality of service that shall be asked of each religious person in God's name. The vow of obedience should be perceived as an active and personalized engagement in one's own freedom. This vow aims to bring our personal wills into harmony with the will of God, as it relates to the mission of the apostolic corpus as a whole and to the complementary involvement of each person who is related to the body.

Religious Life as an Expression of Community

For our purposes, we can dispense with the phenomenon of eremitic life, which, although an early form of religious life, was not a complete expression of it, according to not a few authors. From its beginnings with the desert cenobites, religious life was envisaged as a communitarian reality, lived in some form of community. An overall view of the history of the consecrated religious life permits two statements:

- First, the monastic model that predominated over the centuries was a reference point for every form of religious community, active or apostolic, including non-monastic institutions. This model was incorporated into the religious life at different periods in the church's history. This was the case, in particular, in the institutions that were centered on their own life. They planned and directed their activities with an almost total autonomy in regard to their works. They conceived of vocation and consecration almost exclusively in terms of personal perfection and salvation. Each local monastic community included a fairly large number of members. Access to the community was restricted to "outsiders," whether religious from other orders or laity who collaborated with them in the works of the institutes.

• On the other hand, the most recent evolution of religious life in apostolic congregations made this kind of monastic community lifestyle virtually unlivable. This can be attributed to the considerable reduction in membership per community and to the diversification of their apostolic work. These two factors make it difficult, if not impossible, for community members to find common places and times to meet. To these factors is owed the profound restructuring of the presence and action of men and women religious. Their understanding of mission and of the nature of their apostolic service is much changed, which has brought about a change in their approach to ministry. A number of tasks were restructured by the initiative of the orders, while others were redirected to provide a closer union between the religious apostolate and the local church's pastoral plan and presence. While some ministries came to be shared with the laity, others gradually disappeared as religious men and women involved in them aged and passed away. Community, in both concept and style, was one of the areas that was more directly affected by the post–Vatican II transformations.

Indispensable Aspects of the New Community Profile

The major consequence of this process was a natural multiplication of possible community structures. It is very difficult today to claim that every community within a single order, even within the same country, region, or province, belongs to a homogeneous whole. The problem is now stated less in terms of the outward forms of community and more in regard to the quality of community—its principles, practices, and expressions. What are the basic elements of this community quality? Without pretending to be exhaustive, I shall underline several indispensable qualifications for apostolic religious community at the end of this millennium. The topic will be developed more fully in another chapter.

The Primacy of Persons

Unavoidably, every community member must make an effort to leave enough room for each individual person—as well as the whole group—to grow. This can only be achieved when individuals in a community are valued and accepted for what they are, taking into account, calmly and objectively, their past and present, their values and limitations. This is the basis for working with someone, concretely and realistically. What makes persons potentially communitarian—an inherent quality of every human being—is their openness to relate to others. Individual beings become persons and qualify for life in community to the degree to which they become involved in communities and groups. Every kind of technique and method which is compatible with the consecrated life and which can contribute to the betterment of this relational dimension must be taken seriously and appreciated. Religious community is not possible where this basic anthropological principle is not promoted clear-headedly and continuously.

The catalyst is vocational. A religious community is not a family, neither is it an ethnic, professional, or social group; it is certainly not built on affinity and friendship. A religious community is a group of people who have been called to the same vocation and who understand and live their calling by faith. This theological character of religious community sets the parameters for the relational dimension that the members require to remove every illusion about other ways of conducting their lives and of overcoming conflicts. It introduces persons into a truly evangelical dimension where love and truth walk hand in hand, creating a space for personal relationships that enable the proper exercise of freedom. This makes the construction of justice possible, in the biblical sense of righteousness and holiness, as well as in its social meaning of care and respect for others and for their personal rights. This holistic evangelical perspective is the reason why consecrated communities exist. They also make community visible and help establish the credibility of our vocations.

Mission Is Central

Religious community is not a static and uncommitted kind of life. It is a group of people who have been called and sent to live and work in the mission of Jesus Christ, and to continue it. The structure, then, of the community's apostolic action—as persons and group—must be intimately tied to the christological foundation of mission (see Chapter 2) and community. Evangelization is a particularly "concentrated" expression of mission. Today, at the invitation of Pope John Paul II, evangelization is taking on a critical and also inclusive understanding that is being put together under the name of new evangelization.

Consciousness of Identity

The anthropological, theological, and christological dimensions of community that have been mentioned are common ground for religious communities. It is their *awareness* of their own identity, however, which gives communities their unique distinctiveness within their respective orders, in the context of a plurality of church charisms. This identity emerges as each order and the members of each local community make a conscious and unique translation of their foundational charisms. Translation of the charisms is accomplished on the basis of responsible discernment, faithfulness, and creativity, as the communities perceive, analyze, and interpret the specific context of mission. Religious communities must be concerned for the evolution and change that will ensue from this process. It is an indispensable part of the ongoing, and necessary, updating of community identity and awareness.

Spirituality and Apostolic Praxis

When all of these elements—anthropological, theological, christological, charismatic, contextual—are integrated, communities begin to portray in their lives a specific apostolic praxis as part of an aware and well-founded spirituality. Spirituality is the dynamic orientation of human freedom as it relates to faith, as we shall discuss in Chapter 9. Freedom and faith encompass every aspect of self as well as the relationships of persons with God, themselves, others, and nature. Spirituality, when it is linked to freedom and faith, has to do with life and with the most fundamental aspects of our interior selves. Spirituality brings together theoretical knowledge, practical action, everyday wisdom, and the dedicated lifestyle of individuals and groups.

Praxis is the conscious and intentional energizing of this entire complex for action. By means of praxis, then, we act within reality and upon it. Through praxis we make history, and we give it a sense of direction. A specifically Christian praxis is a life that is guided by the gospel. The root of all apostolic praxis is spirituality. Apostolic praxis, however, also inspires and nourishes spirituality. In the religious life a spirituality of apostolic praxis proceeds from a perception and interpretation of reality in the light of a particular reading of the gospel.

The identity of a religious community emerges, then, from awareness of its apostolic praxis, as it is existentially experienced and discerned in the context of its own spirituality. Prayer is the primary inspiration and source of the feedback of a rightly related spirituality and apostolic praxis. Prayer is therefore the axis that sustains, illuminates, and furthers growth in communities that are founded upon common vocation and consecration for mission.

The Future of Religious Life

It is not possible to cover here all of the important aspects of the consecrated religious life in our day. So it makes sense, before closing this chapter, to reflect about the future of the religious life. We must distinguish between theological and sociological approaches, because each will lead us to different observations and conclusions.

The Future from a Theological Perspective

From a theological point of view, I believe that the religious life today has a solid critical and theoretical foundation with the Bible and theology as its bases. This makes its design and meaning and position distinct among the various vocations of the church. This perspective accounts for the reason and nature of its servant presence in the world and its orientation toward building the Kingdom. The centrality of mission, which is today understood as the root and reference point of all apostolic religious life, clarifies at one and the same time the primacy of christology (the mission of Jesus Christ) and the continuous inspiration of the Spirit in both apostolic discernment and its charismatic and prophetic feedback. Here, from an ecclesiological perspective, religious life is to be found. In effect, mission is today understood in its relationship to real contexts of presence and action. The church is the mediation of this contextualization.

At the same time, as it persists in being sensitive to present reality, post-conciliar religious life nourishes itself spiritually in ancient sources and not only in the immediate present. Historical, patristic, and biblical research are continually rediscovering and reevaluating the spiritual contribution of past traditions for today. We are thus building up an important reserve of formative elements for our time while remaining in intimate communion and continuity with past traditions. Today's religious candidates and novices have at their disposal a fund of knowledge about the consecrated life that was almost certainly not accessible to previous generations. These resources are exponentially increased by the frequent translation and interchange of quality works across frontiers and by the intense rhythm of meetings, seminars, congresses, and chapters at an international level that furthers a noteworthy exchange and sharing, inside and outside of the religious orders.

This succinct thematic overview assures us—from a theological point of view—that consecrated religious life remains significant and pertinent for the church. I would even say that the religious life has sharpened its definitions, deepened its requirements, and has now a better understanding of its own place in the church than previously. We have a greater and more explicit awareness of the nature of the consecrated religious life, and of its implications—biblical and theological, christological, pneumatological, and ecclesiological, charismatic and prophetic, missiological and spiritual. We have the theoretical data at our disposal to define every level of our training projects and to nourish our daily lives.

The Future from a Sociological Perspective

From a sociological perspective all religious orders are burdened with many concerns and questions. First, with very few exceptions, the majority of our religious order provinces around the world suffer from a serious deficit of vocations. From a purely demographic point of view this is quite understandable. In a mere fifty years we have moved from families averaging six to eight children to homes where the average is only two or three. For this and other reasons there are few admissions, in absolute terms, into our orders.

In addition, in spite of all the efforts expended in selection and formation, the departures of professed religious remain relatively numerous. In many places there has developed a judicious and up-to-date pastoral-vocational orientation. The effects of such planning have been positive, but the vital apostolic needs of our congregations and the increasing demand for services that the world expects of the church far outstrips numerical resources. And we certainly are out of tune with many young people. Even when we share ideals and aspirations, there are barriers in communication and approach.

Youth and Religious Vocation

I want to highlight two more factors that contribute to the grave vocational deficit. First, the rich potential of candidates is not in harmony with the deficient and often debilitating upbringing that they have received. The product of broken or problem homes, their mental and psychological growth has often been retarded. We could add that emotional disturbances, deficiencies, and even pathologies sometimes require more than spiritual help to overcome. In almost all of our orders we have today a considerable number of religious who are undergoing some kind of psychotherapy or treatment. This implies major investments of time and money. I am not aware of any easy answers to the problem. I have to ask myself if we have dealt with it adequately and sufficiently.

Second, there is the factor of deficient formation in matters of faith and practice. Truly Christian homes today are few. Homes were for many generations the cradle of spiritual experience and of evangelical aspirations, the source of our religious vocations. The quantity and quality of Christian faith formation has been drastically diminished. Growing secularization in public schools in particular (but in religious schools as well), family pressures, and student resistance seriously hinder religious formation that is significant and germane to the world. Commendable efforts toward a renewed catechesis in our parishes are but a drop in the bucket when compared to the mass of unreached children.

It is, therefore, short-sighted and superficial to attribute to a single factor—the lack of discipline or spiritual weakening of the religious orders is often blamed—the vocational crisis that we are all experiencing. Nor do I believe that transferring young religious from vocationally rich, rural third-world countries to vocationally poor regions in the First World or to cities in the Third World is any solution. Mostly recruited on the basis of pre–Vatican II criteria, they will only perpetuate in other countries works and institutions that would not survive without their presence. Entertaining this option, in fact, shows a lapse of inculturational-theological criteria. It also sets up a failure in the sociological area, above all because the imported vocations face cultural shock and lack the proper training and advice for these situations. They are asked to provide functional continuity without any concern whatsoever for the cultural and emotional shock that they will surely suffer. What makes this so complicated is that it is happening at a time when the orders are moving toward a more inculturated approach to formation and mission.

Aging and Religious Life

Running parallel to the vocational crisis, we are facing a worrisome process of aging on the part of our members. This is not a totally unexpected biological and psychological phenomenon. But the sheer number of people who are simultaneously aging, without corresponding new replacements to reestablish the equilibrium of other epochs, creates the impression that the process is accelerating irreversibly. This impressive phenomenon in developed countries and in a few third-world regions has very practical, institutional, and operational repercussions. It also has notable consequences for the formulation of priorities, the allocation of human and material resources, and even the way in which we structure mission and spirituality. There is no way we can minimize this phenomenon; even less can we overlook it when we think theologically and spiritually about consecrated life and its place in the church. In Chapter 10 I shall give more space to this crucial problem.

Middle Age and Religious Vocation

The lack of young vocations and increase in elderly religious seriously overload the middle-aged generation. The vocational deficit and consequent slowness in reorganizing apostolic services have caused the weight of great institutions, once carried by many men and women religious, to fall upon a reduced number of persons who shoulder enormous responsibilities. This is the combined result of aggravated problems and drastically diminished resources. Simultaneously, this same middle-aged generation is called upon to assume additional pastoral responsibilities—in parishes, catechesis, and many other areas—as orders become more involved in local churches that are in dire need of their services. And it was this very same generation—ranging today between the ages of 40 and 60—that went through the turbulent changes in church and world following World War II and Vatican II. We who went through these very critical and difficult phases were certainly strengthened and grew. They prepared us to meet extremely complex situations. But at the same time they sapped our strength and left us disoriented. Despite all of the retraining courses that are available, the extra workload interrupts the normal rhythm of recharging batteries in community.

During the next decade, many of my generation will be leaving active service, without any backup or replacement. Realistically, this state of affairs forces us to rethink our way of being and doing. We cannot continue to exalt the religious life in the abstract, enchanted with it in theory, but relying only upon alienating theological criteria in our documents and pronouncements. We must keep the social and anthropological complexity of our dilemma very much in mind. We need to approach it with care and courage. The situation cries out for sensible analysis and serious decision-making about personnel and resources. We desperately need discernment, and we need to be lucidly free and spiritually pliant before the Holy Spirit's work.

Conclusion

Within the limits of this chapter we have been searching for a few elements that characterize the consecrated religious life as it presently exists. After a brief historical review of the major post–Vatican II changes, we focused on the religious life from three angles: 1) the perspective of its self-understanding and foundation; 2) the perspective of its internal structures; and 3) the perspective of its community expression. We then looked toward the future of the religious life, distinguishing between a theological focus and a sociological approach. The first approach revealed the considerable richness and a promising outlook for the religious life. The second focus brought us face to face with enormous difficulties. Our grave mistake, on the practical level, as churches and orders, would seem to be that we have not known how to make the proper distinction between these two planes.

The upshot of these discussions is that—while the basic institution of the consecrated life is not really at stake—the problems are real and must be faced. Theological hope and theological foundations confirm the meaning of the religious vocation and mission in its entirety. This is what justifies and gives meaning to the vocation. We have, even more so than in earlier times, something worthwhile to offer, and we have the means to offer it. We are, however, faced with a tremendous challenge as to how to structure apostolic and religious life in concrete situations. We have been given, by the action of the Holy Spirit, the urgent responsibility to find ways to make this happen in our times as we approach a new millennium. Concrete history and life belong to us as human persons, the unique means to attain the eschatological utopia that is inherent to our consecration.

7

Religious Communities

New Problems, New Responses

The religious life as we know it in its history and present reality was preceded by a hermit phase. In contrast to a Christian society and a church that was everyday more influenced by a nonevangelical understanding of life, some individuals from the third to the fourth centuries decided to isolate themselves from the world, to "flee from the world." This shaped their individual lives, and from this framework of austere asceticism came the church's understanding of society.

Hermits also fulfilled a pedagogical function concerning prayer which has lasted down through the centuries. Even today we find here and there individuals who have taken up the eremitical lifestyle, whether permanently or for a limited period of time. They do so to fulfill an inner need for silence and prayerful concentration or to gird themselves for major life decisions. Although an eremitical lifestyle is tangential to some aspects of the religious life, it is not a prototype of it. One cannot say that hermits provided the guiding experience for the religious life.

It is among the cenobites that the first cells of religious life in common began. They are recognized as the initial expressions of the lifestyle and ecclesial vocation that came to be called the consecrated religious life. From the cenobitic model also came the church's understanding since the fourth century that life in community lived under a rule (*regula*) is the elemental structure of the religious life.

Many have been the forms in which religious community has been expressed over the years. But practically until Vatican Council II the point of reference for religious community—even the newer, active communities—was the monastic model. To share time, space, and mission activities comes naturally in monastic communities. The venue is a monastery, a well-defined and identifiable social location. Furthermore, monastic communities mirror the rural and agrarian social context that prevailed before the onset of urban modernity. This accounts for the focus upon times and seasons and the perennial custom of early to bed and early to rise. The rural context allowed for meals to be eaten at set times and the divine office sung or recited together. Liturgical celebrations were elaborate because they were entrusted to monks and nuns, and tacit active participation of the laity was excluded. Despite the laity's appreciative and devout participation in prayer, they were, in fact, mere spectators of celebrations for which they could not provide creative input. Even today there are monasteries located in the heart of large cities that maintain the same schedule and distribution of tasks. It is a vestige of their non-urban origins in the second half of the first millennium and in their apogee during the first half of the second millennium.

Over the centuries, those founders—both women and men—who conceived of introducing innovations to their orders met with considerable ecclesiastical resistance to change. For their part, the enormous concentration of religious in large institutions, founded and operated by the orders, meant that there were significant communities of religious working in so-called apostolic works such as schools, hospitals, orphanages, and so forth. Until the decade of the 1960s, it was not uncommon to find communities of over one hundred members within the great Catholic universities of North America or in traditional educational and health services in Europe. Indeed, this was standard among communities attached to houses of learning. The number of graduates in theology and philosophy that they turned out was proverbial, as were the large facilities that they built and expanded right up till Vatican II took place between 1962 and 1965. When the number of vocations suddenly decreased and a new concept of formational communities developed, many of these large plants were rapidly emptied or recycled for other uses.

Fundamental changes in religious life took place during the decades of the 1970s and 1980s. After almost two thousand years of predominance, the original monastic community model was then seriously questioned as a viable model for mission training and practice in the apostolic religious life. Though it may remain adequate for some forms of contemplative life, one can almost pinpoint the moment when this model of community became impracticable for the active apostolic life. Moreover, it appears that this has occurred not only for today but presumably henceforward. I say "presumably" because the contemplative monastic life is undeniably attractive, especially to men. The boom in monastic vocations in countries like the United States and in the perhaps unique case of the ecumenical monastery at Taizé, France, is important data that must be taken seriously. But for the most part, the time has passed to imagine imposing a monastic model upon communities of the active apostolic life.

The Principal Factors in Change

We can classify the main factors for these changes in the community model of the consecrated, apostolic, and active religious life into three groups—*sociological, theological,* and *anthropological.*

Sociological Factors

The notable diminution in vocations caused, in the span of a few years, a decisive reduction in local community membership. From living commonly in groups of thirty and forty members community size has drastically dropped, in a process somewhat akin to that of what happened to families with lower birthrates. In Brazil, in barely fifty years, the average birthrate dropped from 6.8 to 2.3 children per family. In other countries the indexes are even lower. In Europe, with few exceptions, the average stands between 1 and 2 children per family.

When the size of families drops, tasks in the household are redistributed and mothers and older children join the job market; interpersonal, social, and functional responsibilities are redefined. It took a while for this to happen in the religious communities, but in the end change was inevitable, despite all the institutional efforts to preserve the ancient models. With smaller groups and with people accumulating different functions, common schedules, for instance, became impracticable. And this is only one of the rigid customs from the past that are no longer feasible. When one authoritatively recommends such elements to community as a structural imperative of the religious life—as is now the case in Eastern Europe after decades of heroic and clandestine religious survival—it is important to be clear as to what type of community we are talking about, and what community models are, in fact, viable. The same concerns should be addressed to international congregations, some of which insist upon a single community paradigm for diverse countries and even for entire continents.

With the increase in utilizing the social sciences in the post–Vatican II research in view of chapters of renewal and new constitutions, a better overall knowledge of the historical roots and evolution of the religious life came about concerning individual orders as well as in the great spiritual traditions (such as the Benedictines, Franciscans, Dominicans, and so forth). It became obvious that the standard model of the traditional religious life in community harked back to other times and different realities. Historical research revealed a curious evolution in religious community. During the first three centuries, virgins lived in their own homes, while hermits and cenobites (from the fourth century on) lived in the desert and on the outskirts of cities. Beginning in the second half of the first millennium, and throughout the Middle Ages up until our time, Benedictine monks built great monasteries—self-sufficient villages, as it were—in the countryside and near newly burgeoning urban centers. Mendicants chose to erect great convents in the heart of the cities in order to serve them.

Women in this same period and a little later, for example the Beguines in Flanders and in other parts of Europe, were concentrated in well-defined territories. St. Angela Merici, in the sixteenth century, tried in vain to establish a spiritual and apostolic bond between consecrated women who remained with their families. It was not until the seventeenth century that the Daughters of Charity of St. Vincent de Paul managed to break the strict and enduring cloister model that had been imposed upon women in the religious life. The congregations that were active during the nineteenth and twentieth centuries lived however, for all practical purposes, a dichotomy. They had considerable autonomy and flexibility in carrying out their apostolic ministry, yet their communities maintained a paramonastic style that was rigorously enforced until the beginnings of Vatican II.

The tendency toward immobility in community lifestyles is an endogenous phenomenon, that is to say, it is a kind of imperative that flows from the internal dynamics of community. It is not a mere matter of canonical law being imposed by an outside authority. A good example of this is the case of the Daughters of Charity. The garb, as established by their founders (St. Vincent de Paul and St. Louise de Marillac), was to be the dress worn by the ordinary women of their time. Centuries have passed and the dress became a habit because of the very resistance of the sisters and was unchangeable until after Vatican II. The garb of the Daughters remained the same, although it was completely inappropriate for modern urban life and for the diverse climates in which the group served. Numerous other congregations maintained the same attitude toward their habits. They resorted on occasion to some sort of direct revelation from Mary, Jesus, or the saints as a way of legitimizing the design and material quality of their habit.

There are many analogous examples of rigidified paradigms in particular times and places that can help us to verify two important points. First, there was, in fact, a limited evolution in community models, in line with the times. This evolution, however, took place within the basic monastic paradigm, which remained normative and stable, successfully resisting significant change. Second, the traditional model for religious community became an abstract reference point. Because it was fairly circumscribed, it was elevated to a conceptual construct. Thus projected, monasticism came to be regularly prescribed at the various levels of the religious life—by congregational superiors and central church authorities—and to a certain degree by the traditional image that the people maintained of religious obligations.

In historical terms, however, as monastic congregations were planted in diverse contexts they created demands for new adaptations. Actually, these demands were not met, thus safeguarding the stable conceptual model of religious life. However, the rationale for non-change was no longer based upon the original sociological explanation, but on abstract spiritual and ideological justifications that had no connection with concrete reality. Many of us have gone through the absurd experience of only one or two baths and barely two changes of clothing per week. We were required to wear habits when playing volleyball or basketball, and a hat and cape when we went to take a walk. All of this was justified on theoretical and spiritual grounds until the beginning of the 1960s in places such as Rio de Janeiro where the temperature stands between 95° and 104° (35° and 40° Celsius).

All of that spiritual justification of monastic habits, while apparently innocuous, was unfounded. It was, in fact, a direct result of conditions in the sociocultural situations in which religious institutes were born. The principal traditions were born and shaped in Latin countries of the north Mediterranean coast, and monastic garb was among them, but these customs extended to methods of prayer, work, language, and many other particulars of daily religious life. New responses that other cultural milieus demanded were simply not considered, at least not until fairly recently. I have lingered over these commonplace examples, which for the most part are no longer issues, to warn of the risk that we face today of returning to the past. While the problem is proportionally not as large as it was before, and the changes wrought have been substantial, we need to recognize that the old principles and criteria are again at work among us.

Beyond all of the above, we witness today the disappearance of a determining factor in the past lifestyle of the communities. Until practically the eve of Vatican II, communities that were virtually small independent cities abounded. They were self-contained, offering everything—food production (vegetable and dairy farms), bakeries, shoe repairs, tailors, mechanics, electricians, plumbers, launderers, and every kind of maintenance, transportation, and communication services. A large number of lay brothers and sisters kept all of this going with dedication, competence, and unexcelled expertise. They were veritable pillars of work and of the kind of spirituality and religious life that they practiced.

The decline in vocations and the restructuring of religious life by Vatican Council II led to profound changes in this approach. Virtually all of this work is done today by paid laity. In order to meet their many needs, religious houses have been forced to join the same marketplace of commercial exchange of goods and services as the rest of the world.

Something similar has taken place in the overtly apostolic fields of education and health, which hitherto had monopolized much of the energies of the congregations. At one time, the presence of religious men and women directly involved in teaching and nursing, or in their administration, was outstanding. But the changes here also have been great. In virtually no country in Europe and Latin America can one now find teachers among the religious—not only of the so-called profane subjects such as the sciences and languages, but even as instructors of religion and as pastoral coordinators. Much of this today is in the hands of the laity, including hospital services. These facts profoundly affect the nature of religious community.

Today the orders must make a priority what was once not a major concern for them—training laymen and laywomen. Only if they are suitably trained will the laity be equipped effectively and faithfully to assume the tasks that entail appropriating the spiritual and apostolic heritage of the congregations for whose members they are now substituting. There is a growing reciprocal cooperation between religious and the laity that is also part of the landscape today in our communities. Laity and religious together are serving in coeducational schools at every age and level as teachers, professionals and employees.

Quite understandably, and inevitably, the sharp contrast between what was and what is in religious communities has had a decisive influence upon our understanding of what the religious community should be in this new context. Nothing, however, can be defined a priori or regulated by mere decree. The transformations are too rapid and unavoidable, too profound and systemic. One must observe them, evaluate them, discern them, and pray over them. Only thus will we be able to settle upon certain parameters that themselves will have to be revised and readjusted constantly. We are, in fact, in a new world, and there is no way to rehabilitate or restore the paradigms of past historical situations. Neither can we impose regulations from other epochs or judge or condemn people on this basis. This does not imply laxness or negligence. It may be rather difficult to be a religious man or woman today in a world that is more fragmented and convulsed than in more tranquil times when societies were homogeneous—not even to mention, when they could be structured by clerics and religious themselves.

Until now I have been working with sociological data only. Such data can be verified, measured, described, and ignored only at our peril. Yet it is also necessary to go beyond these facts. It is important that we foster in ourselves an awareness of a much more profound and complex level of transformations. This will always be for us a more trustworthy source of criteria, one that can free us up in the face of all the sociological data so as not to give it undue importance.

Theological Factors

If religious community life has changed externally, even more profound have been the transformations brought about both in concept and image of religious community stemming from internal perspectives. Trinitarian theology awakened the religious life to the double dimension of relationship and of communication in communion. The God of Jesus Christ—Father, Son, and Holy Spirit—is prototype of community within a relationship of love. This is nourished by communion and intense, loving communication among the Persons in perfect unity. The inspirational axis of religious community changed as a result of this awareness. The focus changed from a more juridical, sociological, or functional approach to a community project that is theologically motivated and more profoundly interpersonal. Authentic relationships became an important gauge of the meaning and quality of community life. Simultaneously, a trinitarian theology also demonstrated the inexhaustible gratuitousness of our Lord's love. God became open to others, that is, to us, in creation, the incarnation, through the death and resurrection of Jesus, and through the presence of the Holy Spirit in the church down through history. This history of salvation is totally recapitulated in Christ—the same Christ who calls and sends us as an apostolic body, that is, our communities.

The most recent theology of vocation, as we have seen in Chapter 1, stresses, at one and the same time, an underlying baptismal unity and the diversity of vocational callings. This contrasts with a theology of diversity of ministries, the emphasis of the 1960s and 1970s, which focused mainly upon lay contributions to the predominantly clerical vocation pattern.

In this way, the key pillar of the religious community's rule has been strengthened. Every baptized person is called to a community of faith which is the ecclesial community. The religious life does not bring this about within natural families but in a nonbiological community, which is neither national, ethnic, racial, political, nor economic. This community is not built upon bonds of affinity or friendship. It is founded, rather, upon the calling to a mission which is historical and at the same time eschatological. Mission awareness and lifestyle, therefore, have become a primary gauge of our motivation to the common life. Because this quality can be replicated anywhere in the world, with the necessary adaptations and inculturations, the mobility and uninhibited availability that is inherent in the religious life now take on a new dimension.

There is now a more theological understanding of the eucharist as a sharing of communion which in no way detracts from its sacrificial, sacramental, and memorial dimensions but goes beyond them. This new reading is both direct and productive. It illuminates the social dimension of the eucharist, highlighting the significance and implications of consecrated poverty and dedicated service. This understanding opens up new horizons for the congregations of gifts, talents, and goods mutually shared. Moreover, it enables them to accept gratefully the response and service of so many, particularly of the smallest and most needy. The eucharistic inspiration for this kind of community transcends and makes relative our initial and sometimes obsessive concern for space-time factors. We can now be more flexible about material factors such as temples and rigid schedules.

The eucharist also substantiates a primary requirement: we must remain transparent and truthful, with charity to all people. The difficulties that keep us from translating love into action indicate a structural deficiency in making community come about, even when all other requirements are present. In other words, the eucharist is the soul and inspiration of community fellowship. The eucharist makes community viable and challenges us to live up to its truth. And community provides a way for the eucharist to become authentic. Where community cracks or becomes truncated, where there is community but not a living communion, there we find less of an opportunity for the eucharist to be consistently credible. There may be a formal celebration, but the very act may empty the meaning and implications of what we are celebrating.

It is necessary to train and shape young and not-so-young religious to help them understand the immense and unique implications of the eucharist for community life. If we do not make the effort to teach them, daily eucharist will be a meaningless, legalistic, and obligatory function. The not-so-young, having become accustomed to a disciplined ritual, can take it for granted. While attending the eucharist faithfully, they can fail to grasp its new dimensions and its many consequences for the life of the community.

This complex of theological points of reference—trinitarian, vocational, eucharistic (we have already dealt with the christological and missiological dimensions in another chapter)—must be theologically molded by the spirituality factor. This includes various dimensions— identity and charism, group belonging, the awareness of being inspired by an evangelical and apostolic approach—all of which shape our life and mission as individuals and groups. This helps us to go beyond mere formal membership in a community. We are all to a certain extent invited and encouraged to be sharers of community through the fellowship that we experience in it, a community that is constantly being renewed. Vestiges remain in each individual religious of his or her own founding charism, which is interpreted in unique ways.

We can see the real face of a religious community in the amalgamation of persons with a common spiritual heritage that make up that community. In this sense, a Franciscan community will be different from a Benedictine, Carmelite, or Salesian community. The same blood courses through both parents and children and distinguishes them biologically from others in the population. In like manner, the same spiritual blood flows through the members of an order or religious community. The theological rootedness of spirituality helps us to understand St. Francis Xavier, for example. He lived isolated and alone in India, Japan, and China, yet his faith maintained an intimate and intense communion with a dispersed community, that first group of companions of Ignatius of Loyola. Spread across the globe, they were intensely aware of their unity in communion. They were a community united in mission and in love despite the distances that separated them. If the spirituality of communion was possible in a community that was as dispersed as this one, how much more are we constrained to make common spirituality work within the almost day-by-day interaction of our own proximate community experience.

Anthropological Factors

None of this is strictly new in terms of the history of religious life and of theology. But the emphases are new—what is perceived and above all the extent of the implications that are specific to religious communities today. One cannot deny recent events—we *are* moving from a view of religious community that was more institution-centered to a more theological and spiritual understanding of the nature of this way of life. Within this context it is easier to understand some of the key anthropological dimensions of community.

First of all, even where communities are sociologically and theologically well established, they are, in essence and above all, places where persons meet. There is therefore an indispensable affective component in community. At the deepest level of their lives, all persons need acceptance, recognition, and affection. Real persons need to share their successes and failures. They need stimulus and support and a minimum of interior stability and security.

In the traditional formula of religious community life, most of this was provided, in principle at least, by the institution. Thus personal affective needs were less apparent. This is not the case today. We can no longer put off finding a way to integrate the institutional and affective dimensions within communities that are less structured according to spatial and temporal dimensions. It is no less important to keep in mind the interior spiritual pilgrimage of each person. The impersonal institutional model of the past gave us a static view of persons that fostered the tendency for certain clichés or value judgments about persons to be perpetuated. Such data was duly filed away until a time when it could be used to evaluate candidates for possible nominations or to deal with problems. Around transfer time, classified files circulated within communities of a province; these files often contained frozen information about member religious.

We know today how much people can change over time. Clearly, positive forces can have a decisive influence upon people's lives. They can be motivated to face new and promising challenges, which free them to get a new start on life. We are aware of the immense and profound care with which God deals with them, taking their personal experiences into account, their trials and tribulations, and the secret workings in their lives which mark them for better things. Such elements make it possible for them, as new creatures, to meet higher requirements of new missions. Much of this process is quite discreet and at times barely perceptible. It is a crying injustice to treat people on the basis of old information and stereotypes about them, however valid they may have been in the past, when they have truly overcome them because the God of life, of persons, and of situations has been at work in them.

One of the major qualities of religious community today could be to pay attention to those interior movements that end up affecting one's whole life. Human beings move at different tempos and in different directions. One of the most necessary conditions for the continued health and vigor of a community is a respect for diversity. Doubtless, to build communities upon these principles will be difficult, especially if we compare them to the more uniform communities of the past which, by the same token, lacked depth in interpersonal, community, and social relationships.

Second, the close proximity of religious communities to less favored people led to the creation of communities that are inserted in the reality of the poor. This is a new form of religious life in community which continues to gain a foothold within the church; it has reached a certain level of maturity in Latin America. The axis of insertion is precisely this—the priority of the capacity for openness to others. Such "others" are above all people who are impoverished and marginalized, who lack justice, and who are oppressed. True insertion demands a disposition on the part of the apostolic religious to accept such persons, along with the intention to help them. It requires the capability to work, not with imposed and preset formulas, but with jointly developed models that take the poor and their sociocultural context in all of its powerlessness, insecurity, and instability as the joint point of departure.

An inserted community will, therefore, have a minimum of institutional baggage and a maximum of functional flexibility. This kind of community will never allow itself to become a priority. For community to come about in these terms there must needs be, above all, a theological awareness that is trinitarian and christological, eucharistic and missiological, vocational and spiritual. This awareness is the starting point for a basic community identity, which can sustain it in the midst of the changing situations of the people with whom community members live and work apostolically. In this kind of community what counts is a priority attention to real contexts and a respect for the nature and tempo of its actors. A religious community makes sense only within the reality in which it lives and works, being a part of that reality. When this is missing, communities will not be relevant to an evangelization that meets the needs of our times in situations in which a major segment of the population is composed of oppressed peoples.

Conclusion

This chapter focused upon the apostolic religious community. It followed a gradual historical evolution of community rooted in the dominant monastic paradigm. We came to understand that, despite this model, legally established and stabilized for so many centuries, there have been, in fact, important changes in the forms of consecrated religious community life. These transformations always took as their starting point specific historical situations for which men and women throughout history sought adequate responses. These changes—some repressed, others accepted and incorporated—took place nonetheless while maintaining the fundamental elements of the previous monastic model of community. This continuity within a relative discontinuity lasted until after Vatican II. It was even one of the criteria for approving the conclusions of the renewal chapters and the resultant constitutions that followed the Council.

There is growing conviction that religious communities of apostolic life must remain autonomous in relation to the monastic paradigm. This much desired and growing autonomy is due to sociological, theological, and anthropological factors. They have profoundly affected the religious life and its inspiration for mission and service to the people of God. Without any possibility of exhausting the subject, I have chosen only a few representative elements in each of these dimensions.

These factors should be sufficient to drive home the point that consecrated religious and apostolically active communities are living organisms whose primary orientation is mission. This mission takes place in real contexts of people and societies and is directed toward them. It therefore makes no sense to attempt to restore old historical models of religious community, as if they were the only ones valid and acceptable for today. Neither is there any future in making absolute present forms of community as the only valid models for now and ever after.

Today's consecrated religious and apostolic community must be based upon theological concepts that are always valid and at the same time particularly significant for the world in which we live. This will come about when flexibility in mission is a major source of inspiration. This means that mission is not done in conceptual and abstract terms. On the contrary, as the mission of our Lord Jesus himself showed us, mission today is only viable and effective when it is illuminated by sensitivity to the relevant social and anthropological factors which emphasize the structures in which mission takes place.

8

Third-World Religious Life

A Challenge to the First World

The Stages—The First World and the Third World

I shall not here discuss religious life in the Third World in great detail. Instead, I want to reflect briefly upon third-world religious life in order to gain perspective on religious life in the church and the wider society of the First World. We shall examine it, however, with third-world eyes, which may offer something of a challenge to our counterparts in the First World.

Following the reflective methodology that we use in Latin America, I first want to outline with broad strokes the reality of third-world religious life. I have chosen to highlight such aspects as will help us to situate our topic: *what does the religious life in the Third World expect from first-world religious life?* As the American and Canadian reader will notice, I am considering the First World here from a European rather than from a North American perspective. Nevertheless, there is relatively much common ground that makes some of the following meaningful also for North American religious.

Religious life, along with ecclesial life, can only be seen as part of the real context of the world in which we live. This world, however, is an extremely complex reality, in which vertiginous, surprising changes are taking place. To mention only a few of the transformations—two great world wars and a cold war in this century, a welter of regional and class wars, with the result that nations and peoples that were rent by conflict must now be reconstructed. We remember a world that was divided into two ideological poles—with enormous sociocultural, political, and economic consequences, as well as the recent collapse of this structure as a result of the crisis of socialism in Eastern Europe. We now see the painful birth of a new Europe as an economic and political community with worldwide status and implications. Scientific, economic, and technological developments have been decisive, above all in such fields as electronics, chemistry, biology, astrophysics, and in the all-encompassing fields of mathematics and computer science, with all of their ramifications and applications. All of these factors, exponentially increased by mass information and instant communication, have radically transformed cultural presuppositions based upon humanist and/or Christian ideals, which had subsisted fairly continuously for many centuries in the millennium that is about to end. In other words, our hermeneutic and epistemological lenses—our preunderstandings, meanings, and perspectives—have changed considerably. Our analysis—how we perceive and how we read the data—and interpretation—our hermeneutics—have also been modified, along with the values and criteria that inspire our praxis.

Religious Life and Cultural Change

Many readers are witnesses and some have been participants as well to and in the process of transformation in the church that followed Vatican II, both worldwide and in local churches. In the specific case of religious life, the changes were profound and significant, as we have seen in the preceding chapters. Upon this basis, new opportunities for apostolic presence opened up in response to the exigencies of the people of God and of the local churches.

All of these changes together affect and encompass the totality of religious life—its concept of vocation, consecration, and mission, the meaning and implication of vows and/or service under authority, the shape of the community, and the nature of initial and permanent formation.

Moreover, religious life discovered and shouldered a renewed sense of ecclesial identity. On the one hand, religious opened themselves up to the joint efforts of the church. On the other, they became aware of their own solidary and subsidiary identity in the context of the many Christian vocations and of the reciprocal relations between apostolic presence and pastoral activity. Religious orders worked to improve mutual relationships with the hierarchy and the laity. However, the degree to which the various congregations assimilated this process differs. Fear of risk, of novelty, and resistance to the urgent needs of the neediest and simple folk kept some religious orders from taking on new ways of apostolic presence and service in a challenging and convulsed world.

It must be repeated often that this transformational renewal was not primarily the result of a new conceptual construct, even though it had a theoretical foundation. First and foremost, it was a process that was effectively determined by the impact of reality upon the church and the people of God, and by the religious orders' search for specific responses to this reality in terms of service and consecration in mission. This accounts for the basic directions that the religious life is taking today. It also explains the colligation of faith and culture—a dimension of inculturation—and between faith and society—a dimension of liberation. Both these elements are expressed in the juncture of faith and life with all that this implies for contextualizing—at both personal and social levels—the theological and spiritual, ethical and moral consequences of faith, as announcement, profession, and life.

Faith, Culture, and Society

These dyads, *faith and culture* and *faith and society*, which are expressed in the search to increase the integration of *faith and life*, became decisive in third-world countries, where the majority of the world's population lives. Insertion became an imperative, as religious committed themselves to the neediest of people and to their environment. Little by little they were able to go beyond rhetoric and sporadic visits to a living experience. This led to changes in their perspective and social location and to a new awareness, analysis, and understanding of reality. Religious consequently began to grasp the need to reclaim the suffering and marginalized peoples both socially and culturally. They sensed that the religious life must become deeply rooted in the gospel and intimately related to persons and communities. I have already emphasized that the ecclesial, solidary, prophetic, and preferential option for the poor is a significant indicator of this complex of profound changes. This option was made clear by the Latin American bishops, and it is being shouldered as well by local churches on several continents. Many women's congregations, especially, are practicing this consistently.

In Africa and Asia, sensitivity to the connection between faith and culture predominates. In Africa there is the complex relationship between tribal religions and oral tradition. But in Asia we find the limitless ocean of millennia-old religions with their abundance of written traditions. In Africa, sensitivity to justice issues is maturing both in regard to the socioeconomic and racial discrimination. In Asia, Christianity is slowly becoming consolidated. This development signifies a qualified social presence and an appreciable return to growth in conversions and in numbers of priestly and religious vocations, despite the small percentage of Catholics in relation to the general population.

In Latin America, violence and injustice, material impoverishment, and the breakup of culture continue to catalyze our awareness of implications of a *faith-culture-society triad*. This is the reason why we require an urgent transformation of social structures as a consequence of the very essence of Christian faith and, in many cases, as a precondition for individual conversion. Humanization must become a part of evangelization.

Inculturation and Liberation

Each of these factors has had profound consequences for newly understanding and practicing the foundational charisms of religious communities, as well as for creatively structuring religious life with an orientation to the future. This is more the case in Latin America, perhaps, than in Africa and Asia. The difference between Latin America's prospective outlook and the retrospective approach of Africa and Asia is a function of the latter's need to recover and uphold their rich and living cultural and religious traditions. In Latin America, native traditions were, to be sure, disregarded and dismembered, if not always completely destroyed. The priority task in Latin America is to shape a new world, building it upon different foundations. There must be, however, the utmost respect for the remnants of the indigenous and multicultural heritage of our peoples. What I am addressing here is the need for an evangelization that is truly new and much more profound and comprehensive. This not only implies enthusiastic renewal of means and methods, but it calls for an adjustment of the content of the gospel to the specific reality of these peoples, as well as to their often heroic responses to the challenges they face.

In the three continents of the Third World we are beginning a gradual process of relating the various dimensions we have spoken of—retrospective and prospective, inculturation and liberation. All the while we are making necessary corrections to the earlier paradigms of evangelization that were exogenous, authoritarian, and homogeneous. Daily experience and a different missiological understanding are helping us to discover how and where to engender a truly new evangelization. It goes without saying that this has given rise to a religious life that is new in both inspiration and expression.

The new evangelization and new religious lifestyle are not in opposition to the authentic evangelical experience of a two-thousand-year-old tradition, which the church recognizes and validates. I am talking, instead, about a new stages in our history, one with different and specific contributions. As is always the case in historical processes, particularly so in religious life, continuity is permeated with discontinuity.

These third-world continents must be granted the possibility and even the right to carry out their roles on the stages of world history and of religious life. In line with particular theological and sociocultural understandings and concerns, for many centuries and even until fairly recently, Europe took on the role of shaping evangelization and the religious life. Europe spread its worldview to the four corners of the earth. This was linked to a colonization process that conditioned and shaped the evangelization paradigm and thus the way in which religious life was expressed. So long as a conception of the church endured in which unity was based upon uniformity, a uniform model of the religious life also prevailed. To the degree to which the multiplicity of cultures and the variety in social organization in the world are valued and respected today and are allowed to challenge Europe and the church, a new form of ecclesial unity will be built upon cultural diversity. This will also take place in the religious life.

The church universal will accept inculturation in the light of the incarnation of Jesus Christ. In the same way the religious congregations and institutes will find the way to appreciate diversity and live with it. True, we are only beginning and even lack a clear-cut sense of the parameters for such developments and sufficient experience in applying them. Nonetheless, we must not suffocate this new burst of ecclesial life. Throughout history the Spirit has spoken to us in many ways, yet she certainly did not spend all her energy on the past. She challenges and drives us today to shape creatively the church's present and future—including the shape of religious life—in the contemporary world. This should be a global initiative for which the Third World needs a large measure of understanding and cooperation from the First World, from Europe in particular.

Risks and Benefits in Different Contexts

The religious life—as a specific way of living within the church our faith in the God of Jesus Christ—is being deeply shaken. We face situations that are, if anything, as grave as when the orders were founded. And they are certainly more complex.

We have already seen some of the major tendencies of these changes in the Third World. A number of factors inhibit and at the same time challenge us—our close contact with suffering people, our virtual impotence to resist iniquitous structures, our extreme dependence upon international structures of power and money, and our repressed and always suspect creativity. These factors have led to a new awareness which continually challenges third-world religious vocations. The result has been a conviction, based upon experience, that the Spirit operates in diverse ways, and that the charisms, when they are seen from different angles, are capable of inspiring original and hitherto unexplored approaches.

In the United States and Canada religious life has become increasingly convinced of the autonomy of the secular—that is, political, sociocultural—sphere. Women in particular have been "discovered" and are increasingly affirmed by the legal structures and the professions. The very responsibility that these two nations have in the international economy has led to an increased awareness among North American religious of the nature of world structural poverty and of its causes in the First World. Sensitive and comprehensive matters such as these have had a direct impact upon the nature, meaning, implications, and advancement of the religious life. This has led to more critical and courageous stances, such as passive resistance to a status quo characterized by injustice and discrimination, violence and oppression, both open and hidden.

We discuss below religious life in "Europe." This may call for some explanation, lest by implication I seem to be saying that religious life in North America and Canada is not plagued by many of the problems facing it in Europe. The reason I focus on Europe is that this is the homeland and still the decision-making center of many institutes of the kind that I have recommended be given more freedom for inculturation. As I have said above, I am generally referring to Europe when I discuss first-world religious life. European religious communities are, in fact, largely "national" and "monocultural."

In Eastern Europe, for example, until recently dominated by the political structures that we Latin Americans have called real socialism, religious heroically upheld the faith for several decades. They struggled against a militant atheism that eroded Christian foundations in family, society, and culture in several countries. The fact that there is a majority of Catholics in Poland and Croatia, and that Christianity is rooted in their cultures, guaranteed an explicitly Christian presence in the struggle and has perhaps caused the promising returns in terms of vocations now experienced in these lands. In the remaining countries, however, the religious life, prohibited and clandestine for so long, underwent a serious numerical decline. Also, their continual imposed isolation made it impossible for these religious to keep up with the post–Vatican II evolution, and even less to take active part in it. They could not benefit from the biblical, theological, and spiritual developments that have taken place over the past fifty years. It is a difficult and delicate matter to find a way to help them join this renewal process without making them feel that they are being unfaithful to all that they staked their lives upon in such adverse circumstances.

Religious life in Western Europe, with its rich historical heritage, is much more complex. In Western Europe, however discreetly it is expressed, there is a feeling of superiority in regard to other cultures. This streak of ethnocentricism is what once validated both colonial and neo-colonial projects in economics, politics, and evangelization. These processes involved adaptation, acculturation, and transculturation, but not authentic inculturation. Religious life in Europe today shares in and profits from the enormous material recovery after World War II and from the surge of technological progress during the 1970s and 1980s. This well-being, however, is tempered by the extreme fatigue and aging of its members. Religious activity also seems to be exhausted as a result of the state's takeover of education, health, and social services. These occupations were once filled by religious. In fact, not a few orders were founded to perform these functions as an aspect of their proper charisms. The confluence of these factors has forced the orders inward, focusing their attention upon their own institutions and members. It has also led to an overwhelming restructuring of social presence and apostolic programs in terms of service to the elderly.

It is natural that one should find here a certain amount of resistance to change and a tendency to preserve and stabilize what has taken so many centuries to establish. It is understandable that European cultural hegemony, validated by indisputable leadership in initiating the transformation processes we are discussing, has made religious reluctant to take risks or approve approaches that carry with them a broad margin of uncertainty and a considerable potential for mistakes.

With these observations and reflections in mind, let us now attempt to formulate more direct answers to the specific topic of this chapter: *what does the Third World expect from the religious life in Europe?* From a third-world perspective, what are the principal challenges to the religious and apostolic life in the church in Europe today?

Challenges and Perspectives

It is impossible to treat religious life in Europe and the United States as a whole in a general fashion. In spite of common roots shared with European religious, the cultural sensitivity of the religious in the United States and recent developments there—among the women's orders in particular—give the United States and Canada a somewhat different profile from that of Europe. In order to avoid making constant provisions about the difference between Europe and North America or overgeneralizing, I shall limit my analysis below to Europe. At the level of religious life, the Third World is asking Europe today to take a hard look at its internal identity and external relations and actions.

1. Identity: Faithfulness and Creativity

From the Third World we ask that religious men and women in Europe spend time considering in depth the nature of their European identity today. We hope they will do this in the full awareness of the richness and authority of their tradition and spirituality. We trust that they will thrust out courageously in a consistent response to the reality of a Europe that is both Christian and de-Christianized. It is to be hoped that they will not merely return to methods and structures from the past at a time when the world and its cultures are looking to the future. This does not mean to reject or undervalue the past. Neither does it mean passively and uncritically to accept modernity and post-modernity. On the contrary, I am speaking here of an evangelical and critical reading of modern culture and of its consequences and perversions. One should not ask disingenuously that modern culture adjust itself to a restoration of the past, or to an eventual, perhaps inadequate, renewal of religious life. But above all, Europeans must realize that they are a cultural area that requires creative approaches for its own re-evangelization.

2. Face the New with Courage

From the Third World we are asking that religious life in Europe not allow itself to be defeated and overcome by the aging process. Do not let this be the cause of guidelines that will have the effect of evaluating and restricting youth. We ask that Europe not structure its programs for spiritual life, presence, and apostolic action upon past experiences and outlooks. Europe still has a huge reserve of thinkers, researchers, publishers, and communicators, all of whom carry considerable cultural and historical weight. We urgently need these kinds of persons and groups to lead the way, not closing themselves into a hegemonic and reductionist worldview. This wealth of resources for reflection must not be emptied of life or sterilized for life. We ask Europeans not to flee from tensions and risks, and not to limit the creative potential of those who are honestly searching for truth. We hope that advanced chronological age will cease to be synonymous with maintaining everything that is old, that it not be equated with past certainties which perhaps no longer make sense today. We urgently need people who have the courage to review communication and language, as well as images and symbolic structures, in the church and the religious life. This is indispensable largely because the message as it is being transmitted is no longer relevant to many persons today in the First World, and the same is rapidly becoming the case in other regions and cultures. It is not enough to be clear on concepts, presuppositions, and principles. Nor is formal precision in guidelines and norms sufficient. What is indispensable is sensitivity to life and a constant interaction with it.

3. A Prophetic Voice

Third-world religious ask that European religious be more concerned about the young people who are being coopted by ecologism and pacifism. Its positive approach to nature notwithstanding, ecological awareness in affluent countries is sometimes promoted without awareness that the greatest of all ecological catastrophes is extreme and worldwide human poverty. There will be no global ecology if human beings are not taken into account as active agents in nature, with all that this implies, for human beings are themselves integral parts of nature.

At the same time, pacifism, after decades of ideological militancy, is now assuming a posture that runs the risk of romanticism and alienation. Pacifism is often silent, avoiding or sidestepping the dilemmas and long-term tensions in a fragmented world. A case in point is the former Yugoslavia. This immature understanding of peace smothers conflicts which are undeniable and unavoidable in today's world, conflicts that if not faced up to will make any peaceful solution precarious and deceptive.

Could it be that behind these two movements, pacifism and ecologism, is a sophisticated and disingenuously irenic accommodation of the First World to its own culturally and economically overloaded status quo? If this is true, these two great movements, with undeniable potential for mobilization, can end up frustrating their original promise.

The reality that we face in the Third World urgently requires that we all be frontier missionaries. We hope that the European religious will find the courage to be prophetic. This will not happen unless we return creatively to the fundamental parameters of the gospel and their charisms, daringly reworked and retranslated for our times. Europe today is radically different from that which birthed and nurtured Western Christianity in its sociocultural bosom.

4. A Dynamic Interpretation of Charisms

From the Third World we ask that European religious orders recognize the fact that their continent is the birthplace of a significant number of religious institutes that today operate globally. It was in Europe that the Spirit gave to men and women in other epochs special graces for the well-being of the church in their time. Deeply rooted in the gospel, these charisms were indeed productive. In successive generations they have attracted men and women who have found in them inspiration for their lives and mission to peoples in many lands. Religious families and spiritual traditions grew up around several charisms. All of this notwithstanding, it is crucial that religious life in Europe not consider the charisms as gifts which remain immobile and static. Europeans, along with the rest of us, must be able to understand and interpret the charisms in different, dynamic ways that neither distort them nor break faith with their original vision. Peoples in other parts of the world are being called, in the midst of their own realities, to seek new answers to new problems. We count on Europe to help us; but we expect openness, understanding, and cooperation, not the repression of new initiatives. We need to keep the future in mind. Acceptance of and respect for diversity and new intuitions and proposals are fundamental to the continuance of life.

Looking at the evolution of religious life in Europe—hermits and cenobites, monastics and mendicants, regular clergy and social action and teaching congregations—we can see how fundamental it is not to block the transformation processes of history. Over a long period of time religious life made numerous trade-offs in attitudes and convictions that had once seemed nonnegotiable. The unpredictable action of the Holy Spirit upon the founders and the groups that gathered around them is proof that prophetic creativity can transform from within humanly inspired institutional and cultural molds. When religious orders were both faithful and creative, new syntheses resulted from the tension between continuity and discontinuity. This can be the case today.

At the moment, however, the dynamics of transformation are taking place more outside Europe than inside it. Nevertheless, the greatest part of decision-making is located in Europe. We must encourage an awareness of diversity, an understanding and acceptance of things that are different, which is basic to our own human identity. In order for Europe to understand and appreciate the prophetic dimension in third-world religious life, its religious life must undergo a new prophetic experience within its own reality. Religious life in Europe must open itself up to the unsuspected potential for creativity that is present in the charisms.

It is as vital for European religious orders to adopt this course as it is for them to continue to be generous in support of the Third World and its initiatives. What is the meaning of apostolic life, presence, and action, if it is not prophetic? We need support and criticism from the First World, but more than all, we need trust and community. Still, the kind of critical evaluation that comes down more often than not inhibits our growth, perplexes us, and gives rise to hostility and resentment. Initiatives that make a lot of sense locally are often nipped in the bud. Decision-making centers have not clearly understood the intuitions that were behind many of these initiatives. They have been denied the respect that is due to God's timing in human events, timing that usually does not coincide with the untimely haste of human beings.

5. *Dialogue: Solidarity with Plurality*

Speaking from a third-world perspective, we ask that European religious become full partners in a new dialogue with religious life outside of Europe, especially in Latin America. We ask the ecclesiastical and religious decision making bodies in Europe to concede to religious in the Third World the right and the duty to be different. We want to be allowed to live our own lives as best we can in our own cultural contexts with all their tensions. And we will do so without denying, ignoring, or minimizing our history and heritage.

If we religious can dialogue in this way—in full recognition of our respective identities—we can undertake a broad review of North-South relations that will extend beyond the boundaries of the religious life. We hope that this new relationship will have an impact upon every level of social, cultural, economic, and political life, utilizing every human and institutional resource that religious possess themselves or are capable of awakening in others through their influence, ideas, and publications. This may be the way forward in a grand common mission, in a new alliance of diverse peoples united for the common good of a pluralistic world. Perhaps in this way we can avoid the clashes and power struggles that today undermine us both individually and corporately. If religious can dialogue authentically among ourselves, we may even be able to promote coordinated, even ecumenical, action by churches in every latitude on the crucial matters that affect the future of humankind. In a world with instant two-way communication in so many areas of human life, religious life must become agile and creative. The source of our influence must be our involvement and solidarity, rather than prestige, imposition, or power.

Religious life can become a viable, perhaps ideal, space for an inspired and specific approach to international relations—in a spirit of penitence and reconciliation, of community and love, something the world greatly needs. In fact, religious life can offer time-tested structures that bring together many cultures, races, and societies. Religious orders can bring to the task a wealth of firsthand and hands-on experience in numerous contexts. Because dioceses are territorial and local, they are oriented primarily toward themselves and to each other. But the religious orders, by their very nature, can transcend territoriality even though they are locally established. Religious life has the means constantly to evaluate its praxis from many different angles, profiting from the diversity of experiences of its members. This is, in fact, a positive and valuable contribution to the life of the whole church. Religious life, with its experience of granting relative autonomy to local bodies within a context of global unity, can also help avoid the kind of centralism that suffocates the possibility of true unity in diversity.

6. Intercultural Focus

The religious of the Third World, in effect, invite first-world religious to take part with us in an intense intercultural dialogue, to make every effort to overcome a Euro-American-centered mentality. Let us encourage gospel-based inculturation in its fullest sense. I am talking about going beyond adaptation and accommodation, acculturation and transculturation, approaches that characterized past evangelization efforts and are still being maintained today as missiological paradigms in some North Atlantic countries.

Surmounting a Eurocentric mentality does not imply losing or giving up European identity, quite the contrary. But it does mean that Europe should no longer be the primary, unquestioned, and immutable frame of reference for every form of religious life. This applies to every aspect of life—cultural and social, economic and political, religious and ecclesial. Because of its experience in colonialism and its present criticism of it, because of its internationalism and cross-cultural experience—in Europe and around the world—religious life in Europe has enough knowledge to make it a source for understanding changes that are transpiring throughout the world.

In this context it becomes all the more important to embark upon a more adequate cultural and ecclesial training of the religious that Europe and North America send abroad. Without in any way discounting their generous motivations, it is important that we grant them the time and means adequately to prepare themselves for insertion in the language, culture, society, and church of the peoples and regions which they hope to serve apostolically.

In addition, I repeat that it is not advisable for young religious men and women to be moved from the South to Europe in order to maintain works that are no longer viable or in dire need of local human resources. We have in mind real cases where religious women are transferred from India, Korea, and the Philippines to European countries. Persons who go out to serve freely and with adequate preparation have very different attitudes than those who are uprooted primarily to meet the survival needs of projects that practically have no future.

Just as the Third World received and still needs evangelizers from Europe, Europe can receive consecrated persons from the Third World for the new evangelization. Yet we urgently need to discern the missionary motivations that inspire any transfer of personnel from one region to another. We should not support the kind of timid conformity that avoids making urgent decisions about the need for new ministerial and/or missionary structures. The same must be said about the training processes, particularly initial formation. People should not be culturally transplanted during a stage of their lives when they are pondering their basic religious commitments.

Finally, first-world members of the general councils of international orders need to overcome their "superiority complexes." Quite often, third-world religious elected by general chapters to take part in the central government of their congregations are undervalued, humiliated, and even marginalized. Cultural idiosyncrasies, racial prejudices, linguistic deficiencies, or lack of technical expertise are the usual reasons. Instead, the general councils must gain the capacity to discover and appreciate the potential for creative innovation that is in third-world leaders, who must be given room and encouragement to share the life within them for the benefit of their congregations.

7. Crossing Frontiers

The Latin American church, as is the case in Africa and Asia, is experiencing tremendous vitality and movement, the result of encounters with specific challenges from our peoples, from their overwhelming needs, and of the way in which all this was processed in Medellín, Puebla, and Santo Domingo. This tendency continues in initiatives of proven worth, such as the Fraternity Campaign in Brazil, in the priority of the Bible in religious education, in the base ecclesial communities, and in the joint pastoral plans. It is evidenced also in new sensitivity to oppressed cultures—particularly indigenous and Afro-American—as well as in our solidarity in sharing the struggle with the people. All the above is being theologically processed and put into pastoral practice.

In a context such as this, so vitally alive, a comfortable and static religious life, far removed from risk and danger, is impossible. Our intuitions regarding the implications of the charismatic and prophetic dimensions for the religious life must take this factor into account. Of course, in this kind of situation mistakes can be made and exaggerations are liable to occur. But we must avoid rejecting everything on the basis of occasional mistakes.

It is particularly important not to truncate the dynamics of the situation by discouraging and condemning initiatives from afar without giving us recourse to appeal. Occasional errors do not signify unfaithfulness to the church or to the founding inspiration of the various religious institutes. They do not imply a rejection of authority. Our mistakes are usually the result of imperfect decisions in complex and urgent situations. Most can be corrected. We do not, for the most part, act with arrogance. Rather, there is a full and realistic awareness of the difficulties and limitations in ecclesial and other situations which are part of our everyday struggle for life.

Conclusion

Third-world religious, in effect, ask that the men and women religious in Europe continue to be authentically European, all the more so because of the challenges that Europe faces today. They need the capacity to strengthen inter-European relationships. The new European Union can be an example of a new kind of unity and communion in constructive intercultural relations.

The people of the new Europe must be challenged to take a fresh look at their own history—to be converted, to forgive and be forgiven for past conflicts. Because the history of religious orders covers virtually the same road that Europe as a whole is walking today, European religious should be active participants and not mere spectators of the process.

A new Europe implies, as well, a vast concentration of alternative economic, political, and cultural energy in the world. A new and significant power is about to appear on the world stage, with unmeasurable influence. Religious orders can and must assist this emerging superpower to consider its position in the world. Religious vocations can challenge Europe to set its sights on building peace, justice, and the freedom to dialogue instead of on domination and imposition. From the religious perspective, the goals of this new Europe should be to build a new world order of social and cultural, political and economic, as well as ecclesial symmetry, interdependence, and solidarity.

But if this is to happen, Europe—and the First World in general—must not close in upon itself. Just as Europe launched out to share with others around the world from the abundance of its culture and religiosity, the entire First World must now open itself to receive from those who are seemingly inferior and poor. In fact, the poor can give to first-world Christians the vital capacity to be intuitive and to relate to others. They can become the seed of renewed wisdom and humanity, of a yearning for transcendence and for a full and renewed life. These values have been lost or have faded over the long march toward civilization and rationalism in the First World, the result of which is today's malaise afflicting a complacent and self-centered Europe.

This is the First World with which religious life must contend. There is there an opportunity to motivate and transform, to help grow, in human and evangelical terms. The illusory and impractical idea that North Atlantic nations will somehow return to a hegemonic Christendom social order is deceptive. And there will be no meaningful transformation if first-world Christianity insists upon imposing its own paradigms on the rest of the world, or interprets the global situation only from within its own particular world experience. Change can only take place with the creation of adult European and North American churches that are ethically sound, theologically rooted in the gospel, critically and lucidly at home in the complex world of which they are part. It will come about, finally, by truly mutual relations among nations and peoples, societies and cultures, churches and institutions that see the world as a whole, as a place where there is ample room for an endless diversity. In closing, I believe that the expectancy and the hope, the questions and the challenges of religious men and women in the Third World are relevant to both Europe and North America, which history again gives the chance to renew themselves with the vision of youth.

Part 3

MISSION AND CONSECRATION

Spirituality and Prospects

9

New Directions for a Spirituality
of Mission

Throughout this book I have emphasized the unique identity of consecrated and apostolic religious life within the entire context of the Christian vocation. I have tried to show the intimate connection between vocation and mission. I have insisted that mission—as following Jesus—is above all the act and process of *evangelizing*. It is this, the evangelization focus of men's and women's vocations, that shall guide our reflection concerning the genesis and consolidation of a fundamental spirituality for mission in the religious life.

Pope John Paul II has insistently called us to become engaged in a "new evangelization"—new in passion, in methodology, and in expression. These three dimensions connote, respectively, devotion, pedagogy, and communication; in other words, our motivation, our activity, and our language. The three dimensions that the pope emphasizes have tremendous implications for us religious in relation to our self-renewal and our apostolic action alongside our peoples.

If we look at the way in which the world as a whole, Latin America, and the church have been moving historically, collectively and individually, during the past five centuries, we will notice a significant difference between what the first evangelization did and what the new evangelization should be doing. It is not enough to fire up our enthusiasm, refine our techniques, and adapt our interaction. The reality in which we live, with all of its failures and accomplishments, distortions and perversions, affirmations and contradictions, is complex and also profoundly challenging.

While we remain faithful and creative toward our faith, we need, also, a new structuring of the contents of a new evangelization in relation to the first evangelization. Outlooks and emphases are different. We must urgently revise and reconsider past attitudes and positions, availing ourselves of possibilities that new insights suggest to the church. Many of these emphases are already being incorporated into our post-conciliar evangelization process, particularly in the period after Medellín, Puebla, and Santo Domingo. This is taking place not only on the Latin American continent but in other places. We need only mention the dynamic theological reflection and pastoral action that is taking place among us—in the creative religious life and the maturity of the laity in many forms—to be convinced that a lot of what is new in the new evangelization is already alive and well among us.

This is not the place to explain in detail what I believe should be the internal structure of a new evangelization. In a few words, I believe that we need a new anthropological and theological vision of human beings and a new perspective on the God of Jesus Christ, whom we announce and witness now and in the future. The perspectives of liberation and inculturation must be brought together holistically so that they may suffuse all evangelization. These are not opposing views, and they must be integrated. Furthermore, we need an awareness that this evangelization becomes real—throughout the world—in two interpenetrating sociocultural milieus that are very diversified and complex.

The first milieu is the indigenous cultures, which in the Third World are impregnated with poverty and injustice, oppression and violence which penetrate the very fabric of our cultural formation and of our social reality. We find in this context primarily those among our peoples who are structurally marginalized and in one way or another discriminated against. This is the lot of Indians, peasants, blacks and many women—in a word, the poor.

The second milieu is today's culture, one expression of which is modernity. It is impregnated by a kind of rationalism which is technical and scientific, secularized and ideological, pluralist and hegemonic. Although there are evidences here of a critical awareness, it is somewhat amorphous from an anthropological and cultural perspective. These two cultural milieus are broadly based and touch each other, sometimes by overlapping, sometimes in confrontation. Both contexts profoundly challenge us in regard to how we should structure a new evangelization for today and for the immediate future.

What is needed to make the new evangelization work is *spirituality.* This is the theme of this chapter, as we keep in mind the frame of reference of a new evangelization that I have just outlined.

Throughout this book I have insisted upon the process of inculturation in both evangelization and charism. I have underlined the importance of the identities and traditions of the various institutes while encouraging a common awareness that the consecrated religious vocation is one of the specific forms of expressing one's personal vocation and Christian identity. The spirituality that I shall be addressing here is, in fact, a basic spiritual substratum, rooted in the gospel project and the primary exigencies that underlie subsequent variant readings of the gospel. The latter are more restrictive. They are responses to historical emphases and circumstances—to contexts, challenges, and concrete needs. What I propose here need not clash with the various readings and approaches to the gospel in spiritual traditions such as the Benedictines, Franciscans, Dominicans, and so forth. These have taken centuries to develop. Instead, what we discuss here in the context of theological awareness concerning religious life and the whole of Christian living represents a common foundation for all the spiritual traditions and for every form of Christian spirituality.

The Semantics of "Spirituality"

Spirituality is the dynamic orientation of human freedom toward faith. Both freedom and faith encompass whole persons, who are both individuals and beings that relate to nature and material objects, to other human beings, and to God. Spirituality, then, has to do with life, and even more basically, with *our* lives. From an explicitly Christian perspective, spirituality is the conscious orientation of personal or collective lives toward communion with other human beings and with the God of Jesus Christ in the power of the Holy Spirit. Spirituality is the implementation and translation of faith into everyday life situations. As is the case with every kind of spirituality, Christian spirituality does this within a concrete, appropriate symbolic structure and a specific linguistic tradition.

The source of basic Christian spirituality is the christological heart of the gospel, with all that it reveals of the mysteries concerning God, human beings, and the world. Faith and freedom must, therefore, be linked to these interrelated mysteries. To be sure, we can only grasp scraps of truth—certainly not the whole truth—about each and every one of these mysteries.

Further, this basic Christian spirituality has been refracted into a variety of approaches and shades—responses to the questions that are being asked again in various times and places. In fact, spirituality emerges from concrete expressions of life, while it inspires and guides the people who are experiencing that reality. This is why we can talk about several spiritualities, and we can even identify streams and schools of spirituality within the wider unified context of a basic Christian spirituality. Some spiritual traditions have had greater impact and lasting influence, while others have not. Some spiritualities have broken with their original charisms; others have had ups and downs, periods of renewal and creative return to their roots, and diverse vicissitudes in turbulent times.

Spirituality has a way of bringing together theoretical knowledge and existential wisdom succinctly. This is why spirituality begins where people stand together without pretenses. We can always find room for improvement. We can be freer and live our faith better. Relationships with God, others, nature, and ourselves can qualitatively mature beyond our wildest expectations. This is the stuff of our everyday life in the Spirit.

The Spirituality of the New Evangelization

Keeping in mind some of the basic prerequisites for a new evangelization touched on above, the corresponding spirituality must be radically evangelical. *This spirituality must be imbued with an ethos of incarnation-inculturation, salvation-liberation, and communication-communion.* This triple thrust is based upon *life* as the heart of living spirituality, the ultimate goal of mission. This spirituality does not clash with particular spiritualities that have grown over the centuries and that tend to emphasize this or that aspect of gospel understanding and practice. Such particular spiritualities often undergird various inspirations that enrich lay and priestly religious life in the church. A number of these spiritualities have become theologically elaborate and have acquired a rich symbolism. Yet there is no clash between them and the basic spirituality that we are talking about. They have, in fact, been interacting constantly. This can increase within the new understanding of evangelization we have been discussing.

A Spirituality of Incarnation-Inculturation

Evangelizers are called to translate the original christological mystery into everyday life. God became human without in any way ceasing to be God. Jesus takes on human reality as it is (Jn 10:36), with all of its sinfulness, even though he remains sinless (Heb 4:15). God is fully God in the incarnate Word, even though in Jesus any explicit manifestation of the divine form is abandoned (Phil 2:5-11), and God is revealed in human nature. As the Council of Chalcedon reminds us, we are faced here with a unique and unfathomable reality: one person with two natures, distinctive and immutable, indivisible and inseparable. The tension between the two natures, in fact, pervades the entire life of Jesus and the New Testament, and projects itself upon ecclesial reality for all time.

Religious always bring their original formation—within unique cultures, biological families, national matrices, spiritual traditions, and the particular orders to which they belong—to evangelization. When they are also part of other ecclesial contexts, they bring with them also marks of their local churches. They continue to be themselves as evangelizers, while their personal attitudes and actions are influenced and changed by the persons, groups, cultures, and societies that they are evangelizing. This is what inculturation is all about. As I have repeatedly stated, inculturation is an integral process of evangelization built within the culture of those that are being evangelized, that is to say, on their terms and in harmony with their cultural traits. It is only in this way that evangelization can avoid transplanting an artificial ecclesial model that reflects other contexts. Rather, it should foster the genesis of new realities, of cultures that are renewed through the power of the gospel, of renewed versions of the universal church, each with a unique identity as new ecclesial communities.

As in the incarnation of the Logos, the faith-culture dyad, with proper relations and interaction, will always keep the divine and human dimensions in dynamic tension. As with Jesus, in inculturation the *divine* element is *humanized*. We receive the content of the gift—God in Jesus Christ—within our own humanity and personal identities. We strive to be faithful to this gift, yet we are unable to plumb its depths. Simultaneously, the human element becomes divine. The gift of God in Jesus Christ moves us beyond our humanity—to a new relationship with God, and beyond our individuality—to a new relationship with others, in full awareness of our limitations. The dynamic of the incarnation-inculturation spirituality reveals to human beings the meaning of their lives—their limitations, present and future possibilities, and their potential for greatness and unlimited growth.

In the context of the incarnation, it is important to discern and grasp the role of Mary as an instrument of the Spirit. In the providence of God, she played an indispensable part in helping the mystery—the humanization of the Logos in incarnation and inculturation—become concrete. God freely chose to work through her for the fulfillment of his loving project on our behalf. Mary was the first to educate this child who was the Word incarnate as well as her son. She introduced Jesus into the nuances of their culture and age.

Incarnation and inculturation are in some ways similar to the conversion process. Belonging to particular cultures—biological and spiritual families, ethnic groups, and so forth—evangelizers become incarnate in a host culture. In this sense also, they are reborn by the Spirit, as Jesus indicated to Nicodemus (Jn 3:3-21). To enter the Kingdom they must become children (Lk 18:15-17). They learn to speak a new prophetic and evangelical language, as in the case of Jeremiah (Jer 1:4-10). The essence of incarnation and inculturation is a spirituality that is theological, christological, pneumatological, and anthropological. Without this, a new evangelization will not take place. It is the ethos that pervades the whole being of the evangelizers so that they are new creatures (Gal 1:15-16).

A Spirituality of Salvation-Liberation

Incarnational theology finds its meaning in salvation-liberation. The entire history of Israel is tied to its experience of liberation. The life, words, and deeds of Jesus—above all his death and resurrection—are facets of the fundamental sacrament of total and full-orbed salvation and liberation that he came to bring us. This includes redemption from sin, freedom from oppression and discrimination, from marginalization and injustice, as well as from every other violation of freedom that human beings inflict upon one another. Jesus made a clear option for people who were in need of liberation: the sick, sinners, women, children, followers of oppressive religions, the poor, in sum, those people whom society, culture, or religion repress, manipulate, and ignore.

The liberation that Jesus brings does not substitute one oppression for another, as is the case with so many liberations in history. Jesus' liberation introduces a radical freedom. It is the "re-creation" of a human identity in which freedom emerges as the central axis. It is freedom with respect to all creation, and in a mysterious way, freedom also in relation to God, a freedom which human beings can either accept or reject.

In a new evangelization the evangelizers shall be witnesses to the liberating action of the Spirit as well as collaborators. There is a redemption from sin which can only be the exclusive work of God—it is the free gift of God's forgiveness, the surprising proof of divine love. But sinful structures that are created by persons who seek to destroy the divine project must also be transformed. This is a kind of liberation in which we can and must play an active role and to which we are called by the very nature of our faith. Transformation thus understood is the responsibility and work of human beings in history, guided by the Spirit and in obedience to the ethical principles of the gospel. It is essential that evangelizers allow the death of Jesus Christ and the new life of his resurrection to awaken new life in them and in their cultural milieus.

Meanwhile, evangelizers can become either instruments of this liberation or hinder it. But they must become free and transparent themselves if life is to shine through them. Inculturated evangelization does not signify the death or repression of the evangelizers or of their cultures. To the contrary, they are freed to transcend their existential limitations, keeping in mind that each person and each culture is only one among many. Evangelizers can overcome their moral limitations—the evasions, perversions, and sins that pervade every sociocultural context. Finally, they have the freedom to discover a more fulfilling theol-

ogy, both personal and cultural, and to be enriched by the new life that
is a gift of God in Jesus Christ.

Within the framework of liberation, the spirituality of a new and
inculturated evangelization must find room to exercise a critical and
discerning awareness. These qualities are essential to bringing together
faith and life, to integrating inculturation and liberation, in response to
the demands of faithfulness to God and to humankind. We need discernment about the authenticity of our mutual relationships, concerning
our communion with God and with each other. In terms of inculturated
liberation and liberating inculturation, we have three specific sources
of inspiration for discernment of the evangelization process: 1) the relationship of Jesus to his own culture; 2) the cross-cultural practices of
very early Judeo-Christian communities; and 3) Paul's explicit theological approach to pagan cultures.

Spirituality of Communication-Communion

Every culture is a system of producing the meanings, values, and
precepts that underlie human actions and communication. All our cultural relationships—whether inward or outward directed, or conditioned
by economic, political, or social factors—are also "communication relationships." Every evangelization process that draws diverse people
and cultures together necessarily establishes communication relationships, even though, paradoxically, these may eventually lead to a precarious noncommunication. In order for there to be meaningful communication between sources and receptors, words, expressions, gestures,
signs, rituals, and codes must be mutually intelligible. Both participants
must find a common repertoire of meanings and signs (words) that are
joined together by shared rules (syntax), so that language can become
intelligible.

Evangelizers, then, must be persons who are open to two-way communication. For viable communication to happen, they must apprehend
and assimilate this lexical-syntactical synthesis and make it their own.
*In evangelization, communication starts with and develops within the
culture of the receptor, not with the evangelizer.* Evangelizers, accordingly, should try to become culturally bilingual, as thoroughly conver-
sant in the idiom of the receptor culture as they are in their own cultural
idiom. Evangelical idioms and symbols must be encoded into the idiom
of the receptors, the people that are being evangelized. This presupposes that for new evangelization to be both liberating and inculturated
there must be an ongoing process of learning new cultural idioms. This
can only take place when a *kenotic* process proceeds—and that includes
a self-emptying of all vestiges of domination, superiority, and ideology,
which have characterized much of our evangelization. In addition, be-

fore we can encode the gospel into other cultures, we evangelizers must be critically aware of the limitations and distortions in our own cultures.

This shared attitude of constructive criticism between source and receptor is what makes communion in communication possible. Effective affective insertion in the context that is being evangelized is also a fundamental precondition for an evangelization that leads to communication. This kind of evangelization is built upon mutual love and appreciation, upon reciprocal trust and esteem. These elements are indispensable if the communication, people, and processes are to be credible and trustworthy; and even more so, when evangelization challenges cultural values and social structures, when it demands conversion and transformation, even to the point of requiring painful disruptions. In principle, communication could limit itself to the mere transmission of knowledge. Communion, however, while keeping this aspect of communication in mind, transcends it and places communication on a plane of total dedication.

Communion is love. It is important in evangelization to seek, discover, and follow truth in love. This spiritual attitude of communion in communication must characterize the spirituality that undergirds the new evangelization. There will always be elements of culture that cannot be communicated or fathomed; there will be intentions and messages that cannot be deciphered. It is at this point where we are called to step into the shoes of the other and to accept the other in a dialogical relationship. No matter how deep may be our unity and communion, love, dialogue, and communication always presuppose that we are different. Conflict is often the price that we have to pay to learn that we are different. But a sincere desire to communicate in communion can help us overcome our differences dialectically instead of making them drastically worse.

Communion in communication is the basic foundation of inculturated evangelization, as it is also for ecumenical relationships among churches, and the more recent dialogue with other religions. Unfortunately, this does not mean a total absence of accusation and confrontation. And in such situations it is not always possible to remain neutral. There are truths which we cannot compromise or ignore. Some situations are radically incompatible with the evangelical message and Christian praxis. At this point our witness can become martyrdom, which over the centuries has been the christological mark of evangelization. The spirituality of a new evangelization must also prepare us for this possibility.

Life as the Foundation of Spirituality

The four dyads—anthropology-theology, incarnation-inculturation, salvation-liberation, communication-communion—that I have suggested are at the root of the new evangelization, are "life-bearers." Other dyads—pre-evangelization-evangelization, direct evangelization-liberating promotion, and plan of creation-redemption, for example—are also involved. Similarly, various dichotomies—natural-supernatural, history-eschatology, earthly-heavenly, sacred-profane, individual-people, persons-communities, and others, become relative and less important. They often make our theological walk difficult. Life evolves and takes shape as we recognize the diversity that is implicit in such paired words. At the same time, life is affirmed to the degree in which we are aware of the possibilities in these word-pairs for unity instead of an otherwise almost inevitable conflict. Sterile conflict leads only to barrenness and death. When we encourage the interior life of individuals—without regard for their social and material condition—we introduce and foster a dualism that impoverishes and suffocates life.

Jesus is life. He came to give us life and life in abundance. The Kingdom which he announces and brings is life. It is this Kingdom that we must, together with him, build in the power of the Spirit. The great mission of evangelization is to proclaim and share this fullness of life. We must build and shape this Kingdom of love, freedom, and justice among those who are being evangelized. Furthermore, when we evangelize we celebrate life as a service of hope within culture and society, as well as in every person in history who is guided by an eschatological hope. This radicalizes every dimension of human life, both personal and social, and shapes life in accordance with the gospel. This is what it means to evangelize.

If we are to share this life with others, both the evangelizers and the people or communities that we are evangelizing must be willing to renounce our lives and respective cultures. We can do this only if we have the critical capacity to analyze, guide, and improve our cultures, if we are capable of not imposing them or making them absolute. The gospel deals in many ways with the theme of renunciation. This quality is supremely fulfilled in Jesus Christ, the giver of life, through his death and subsequent resurrection.

Conclusion

There is a fundamental economy of "gratuity" in the entire evangelization process, that of constantly *giving without expecting a return*. This economy of giving pervades creation, incarnation, and the entire history of humanity—the history of salvation. This gratuitous element reappears in inculturation, liberation, and communication. It is the foundation of communion. It is life, always available, inexhaustible, and full of the power of life—which is gratuitous in its inmost structure.

As it was with Jesus, this is the proper mission of evangelizers. The spirituality of the new evangelization is deeply rooted in mission. It is inspired, shaped, vindicated, and motivated by mission. It is a spirituality which is nourished by the centrality of Jesus' mission as it is continuously translated into the mission of the church by all of us. Every Christian, and in particular men and women religious, is continuously called to this apostolic effort. We are called by the Spirit to a new evangelization of ourselves, first of all, of our brothers and sisters, and of our churches and communities as we come to the end of this millennium. The specific spiritualities of our orders must follow this path. They must never center exclusively upon their individual sanctification and growth, but be always oriented toward the vast horizon of mission. This is the reason for our existence, first and last.

Mary is the living icon which carries forward and inspires this spirituality. The human potential for life in her was divinely impregnated by the Spirit, perfected in a life shared with Jesus, a life which he now offers to us. "Behold your Mother!"

10

Religious Vocations

Principal Elements of a Way Forward

Let us now attempt to bring together some of the key issues that I have highlighted throughout this book. We will focus upon the problems, challenges, and present opportunities for religious life in the West. With the diversity of situations in which religious find themselves, I cannot generalize worldwide. However, the international orders are spread over the globe; consequently, what I shall say will either reflect or affect, at least in part, the reality of many congregations.

Survival: The Shadow and Extent of Uncertainty

At this moment some religious orders are facing a survival situation. While, with the exception of several institutes, most communities are not in imminent danger of closure, the matter of their survival must, nonetheless, be squarely faced with serenity. We should not expend all our precious energies on this problem or allow it to get in the way of efforts that should be directed toward our future mission and vocation. But neither should we keep quiet about the facts that affect our survival, nor should we ignore and minimize them, nor avoid thinking seriously enough about them. This would be as irresponsible as not to treat a potentially terminal disease.

Four factors are in evidence. We do not need to document or prove them statistically, because all of the data is more than familiar to us.

There is first a *sociological factor*. Our membership is growing considerably older, with all that this means in terms of requisite care, increased costs, and fewer persons available for apostolic ministry.

Second, there is the *demographic factor*, which is one of the partial indicators of the sociological factor. In the urban and metropolitan areas of the First World and Third World, a noticeable decrease in birth rates has resulted in a reduction in the number of potential candidates for the religious life. Even in the developing nations, the number of people who reside in urban areas is rapidly outnumbering those that live in rural areas.

Third, there is a *pedagogical-pastoral factor*. We have already emphasized that family, school, and society are being greatly affected by the consequences of Western modernity and are no longer favorable environments for encouraging religious vocations.

Fourth, there is a *symbolic factor*. On the one hand, in the environment of family and school, society and culture in which we live, religious life has lost much of its visibility, intelligibility, and appeal. The major source of information today is the mass media, especially television. The presence of religious there is infinitesimal, and what is portrayed are often unattractive, outmoded, and distorted images. On the other hand, religious often encounter themselves as perplexed and without answers to the external and internal problems that we face. This serves to diminish our self-understanding and confidence. We see our identity partly disfigured in relation to the well-defined paradigms of the past. Aware as we are of the ambiguity of our own identity, we are hesitant to attract new vocations to a lifestyle we love in a present that we fear and a future we cannot clearly see. These facts raise several issues and questions.

Aging

Clearheaded, constructive attention to the aging religious among us is fundamental. I presuppose that each of us needs psychological and spiritual preparation for this phase of our lives. Only in this way will we avoid the premature biological and psychological decline of our people. Only in this way will the potential for life and service in community be optimized, encouraged, and appreciated. We need the resources that science and technology can offer, as well as the instruments, methods, and processes that we religious men and women have yet adequately to create. Information exchange among congregations and institutions that are involved in experiments or who have found workable solutions is important.

If we make such provisions for the benefit of our elder religious, with care and realism, the phenomenon of aging members should neither monopolize our attention nor become the main criteria for the way in which we conceive religious life. Above all, we must not allow this to get in the way of our apostolic freedom. Consecration and mission must be conceived and lived intensely in the present, with eyes focused upon building the future. While we maintain our roots in the past and in our heritage, we should not allow them to condition or to suffocate us.

Community as an Apostolic Body

We must urgently restructure our apostolic action, keeping in mind two elements: first, quantitatively smaller communities; and, second, openness to persons who are especially sensitive to our apostolate and community. Let us take these elements in turn.

Realistically, we must accept the formation of communities that are quantitatively smaller as a result of the sociological factors discussed already. We are experiencing a time of divestiture. A wider spectrum of persons, as in the past, would of course provide us with greater opportunities for excellence and competence. However, we need to learn to live humbly with our loss of self-sufficiency. We must train ourselves to complement each other, to involve the laity, and to join other congregations in a variety of common projects.

None of the above will happen if we remain unwilling to re-educate ourselves and to do so in ways that contribute to healthy interpersonal relationships. This attitude should flow from the awareness of community members that we are an apostolic body that is engaged in common mission, even when individual persons carry out different functions in different places. This awareness is crucial for greater clarity concerning our vocation and mission. It can also foster the kind of visibility that is needed to challenge others to share in our life and mission. Qualitative sharing among people should inspire and nourish further interaction between the orders, as well as their own relationships with a variety of pastoral initiatives.

Apostolic communities should be open to persons who, through faith and the work of the Spirit, are sensitive to evangelical generosity and loving service. Instead of closing themselves within isolated and protective ghettoes, our communities should become sources of joy and hope. Religious communities must remain faithful to what should be and respond creatively to the challenges that they face. This will help vital people among us, as adult members of the community, to have the environment and gain the disposition necessary to carry out mission in ways that will draw younger people to a life consecrated to the Lord and to the church at the service of the people of God.

We can also encourage *lay collaborators* to join us in mission. They can share our responsibilities and tasks, all the while growing in our charisms and spirituality. This cannot be improvised or put off. And it isn't a one-way street with us religious dictating to the laity what they must think and do. We are talking about reciprocal relationships, wherein we become open to learn from the laity and receive suggestions and advice from them, while we share with them what we can.

These two points must become priorities. We should neither overlook them nor smother them in abstract rhetoric—the typical procedure in religious life, a kind of praise that attempts to motivate us but sidesteps concrete and urgent problems. For this to happen, we need to develop means and tools to train religious as well as the laity who work together in mission. We urgently need a company of shared growth that can enable the laity to become knowledgeable about the sources of our inspiration and the criteria of our spiritual traditions. The laity can no longer be treated as extra help. They are authentic collaborators with whom we share the same spirit and common goals. In this handful of survival-related elements I see three disturbing points at issue.

First, there are many volunteer young people who offer a solid portion of their lives to mission. Many of them come from the First World to serve the Third World. Many of them are exposed to difficult cultural adaptations when they go abroad. They must, for example, learn new languages and risk picking up exotic diseases, while they give up even the most basic necessities of hygiene and comfort. I have also noticed that a significant number of young people are deepening their faith in meetings, retreats, and camps with a spiritual orientation. This pastoral activity among youth has mobilized tens of thousands of young people among us. Despite all this, it is disturbing to note that few of these dedicated youth think about the possibility of an apostolic religious vocation in response to the abundant grace that they have received.

Second, I am intrigued by the fact that a surprising number of young people are joining congregations that have not changed or have returned to pre–Vatican II spirituality, discipline, methods, and symbols. While the motivations for this are quite dissimilar in the First World and Third World, the same phenomenon is at work in both regions. I have also noted a peculiar phenomenon that has occurred because of the unexpected changes in Eastern Europe. Until recently, there was an abundance of vocations, especially in Poland and Croatia, places where the lifestyle of religious was different from that of Western Europe and North America. One could, perhaps, single out a variety of dubious motivations—such as escape from harsh domestic reality, insecurity, intellectual needs, and social advancement. These factors, of course, were present in many orders in pre–Vatican II days; they may still be present in a few countries. Nonetheless, the fact that religious life appeals to persons in adverse sociopolitical and cultural situations should make us wonder about the evangelical quality of our own lives. How authentic and transparent are our commitments? Is there consistency between what we are and what we do? How do we see our own identity? Are we clear about the direction and attainment of our apostolic mission?

Third, in the urban Western world, the persons who are seeking admission to religious congregations are older, better prepared, more self-contained and self-reliant. A few younger persons are choosing to join our congregations, but not many. Spot-checking, I have noted that a good crop of candidates is admitted, but a high proportion leave after a short time. We keep hearing that young religious men and women who come to us with new experiences find little room to practice what attracted them to the consecrated life in the first place. Disillusioned with the path they chose, some leave. Others adapt to the established rhythm of the communities, but their pristine motivation loses much of its luster. We should be profoundly disturbed by evidence of such tension and the frustration and dissonance that it causes and reflects. At the same time, we should not overlook the fact that sometimes the weakness of the original motivation for entering is revealed over time to be a problem for the orders. Such candidates often are ideologically restless and financially prodigal, problem students, lax and superficial. They shock the older generation that has survived economically and spiritually difficult times and that has been surrounded throughout life by demanding and competent religious and professional role models.

"Crisis" in Religious Life?

As we reflect upon topics that have to do with the survival of religious institutes, we can ask ourselves whether the religious life as such is "in crisis." The answer, I believe, is yes, provided we rigorously define the term *crisis*. Crisis is a tired term which today has mostly negative connotations. It once signified grave situations, difficult, rending, or unstable moments, nonviable periods, or serious impasses. Crisis, however, is a key technical word that designates the process which underlies profound transformation. It is a phenomenon which is inherent to the human condition. From an anthropological or cultural and psychosocial perspective, *a crisis is a situation or circumstance in which a historical system (for example, a society or culture, an institution or enterprise) reaches a point where the cumulative effect of internal contradictions makes it impossible to resolve problems and dilemmas by mere adaptations or adjustments and to maintain the accepted framework of its principles, criteria, and institutional models* (I. Wallerstein). A crisis is a situation in which one of two results is certain: 1) deep transformation will take place; or 2) the historical system will decline and disappear. As a result, those who make up the system, direct it, or take part in it, are faced with a real choice and an unavoidable decision. *What kind of new historical system must we create or build?*

Let us take religious life as a historical system, in the sense that we used it above in our definition of crisis. We can objectively say that it is in crisis. This is an honest and likewise positive assessment. It neither camouflages a situation which, from our own experience, we know to be serious, nor does it give up in discouragement. Whether consciously or unconsciously, we religious are aware of being in a crisis state. Therefore we should accept as constructive the various stages of significant change that we have lived through since the Second Vatican Council. We should be filled with hope, despite the uncertainty and confusion that we are feeling. This critical stage requires that we take a hard look at the processes and changes that are taking place in the reality in which we live, as well as in our own lives. This is the only way in which the religious life can be defined in terms that are adequate to our age and to the demands of contemporary mission, while remaining worthy of consideration by potential members.

The numerical membership reduction in the religious orders and congregations has happened several times in history. This fact has been well documented by Raymond Hostie in his book *Vie et mort des ordres religieux* (Paris, Desclée de Brouwer, 1972). The author points out, however, that the causes of the reductions in the past were mostly extrinsic to the orders—such elements as disease, religious strife, or wars between countries. Other causes were the influence of kings and princes, which was based upon the post-Reformation principle *cuius regio eius et religio* (freely translated as "the nation follows the religion of its prince") and papal decisions (such as occurred in the case of the suppression of the Jesuits and their 23,000 members in 1773).

Such external factors, however, do not determine our present-day diminution in numbers. What is at stake is a complex set of factors and changes in society, culture, and church which affect the very life of the religious, as well as the way the orders are perceived and evaluated by others.

Over the centuries external and internal factors have weighed heavily in the creation, maintenance, and transformation of the paradigms of religious life. To rehearse once again the outline of major paradigms in the history of the religious life, the monastic model was followed by the mendicants, they by the regular clerics, who in turn were followed by the societies of apostolic life. Of interest is the fact that the creation of new paradigms did not mean the extinction of those that preceded them. Rather, a kind of discontinuity in continuity obtained in which the basic models survived down to our own day.

Hostie makes it clear that the institutes that succumbed to the transformation process were generally those that simply turned to the past to reaffirm blindly their charisms. In other words, they remained materially faithful to the past but did not heed the challenges of their own age. Quite the opposite was the case with those that survived and were renewed. While these remained faithful to their foundational charisms, they managed, nonetheless, to relate them to the demands of their present at a new stage of history. They offered adequate, convincing, faithful, and creative responses to the new challenges, and so they lived on.

I believe we find ourselves today in an analogous context at a crisis moment in religious life. The survival of our institutes will not come by simply restoring the past. This tempting way out carries with it the seeds of its own destruction, which sooner or later will become evident. It will not be able to resist the all-encompassing and systemic historical processes that we are living through. Congregations that have become immobilized or that are tied to an age that no longer exists will continue to experience crises that are identical to those that they were subjected to after Vatican Council II. These crises persist today, but at another level. I believe that the survival and the apostolic significance of institutes derive from their capacity to keep before them the complexity of the world in which we live, with its specific demands, and the subtle and comprehensive scheme that lies underneath it. It is indispensable that we keep in mind the structural coordinates of our reality so that these problems can continue to be linked to the meaning and possibility of our own survival. Many other problems are linked to this basic issue. And much of our apostolic future depends upon an adequate focus and treatment of it.

Identity as a Challenge to Religious Life

Identity is the central challenge posed today to religious life. We must remember that it wasn't too long ago that we were assured, on theological, ecclesial, and sociological grounds, of a privileged religious life among other church vocations. We believed that we had a quasi-monopoly on holiness as a vocation, since religious life was supposed to be "objectively" the most perfect evangelical state of life. This perception legitimated our pastoral independence and resulted in a religious life that was strong in works, self-assured in a homogeneous world. We did not lack internal and external support from many quarters. All of this was couched in easily identifiable symbolic language, but rather than drawing us closer to God's people and their daily reality, it separated us from them. So long as this state of affairs endured and was the key to interpreting religious life, we were not overly concerned about identity. We assumed that our identity needed no other affirmation than our stylized and codified way of acting and proceeding. Formation could be carried out in well-defined and established ways.

Theology and the post–Vatican II evolution put a large question mark on all of the above. By the same token, it opened the way for us to begin a new and ongoing search for our identity as religious. To speak today of identity does not in the first place signify an emphasis upon the things that separate, distance, and alienate us from others. It intends, rather, to help us discover our place as one vocation among other vocations. This should help us to grasp the complementarity of diverse vocations in the ecclesial community—including the complementary and integrating roles of each vocation. This means that we shall not be identified primarily by the way we dress and work, by our lifestyle and buildings, by the strict hours that we keep, or by how we relate to one another. In a world that is structurally secular and pluralist, the crucial points of reference and identity are not phenomenological. In such a world one only finds self-identity when one discovers the meaning of one's life and mission in the context of the world and human existence—ultimately in a theological and ecclesial perspective. Therefore, *the identity of consecrated religious life is found primarily in anything that helps us to recover the fundamental marks of Jesus Christ, who is the cornerstone of all that we are and seek to manifest.*

This is the sense, the direction, and the reason for being of lives that profess publicly their determination to be evangelical. With all Christian men and women we are called to follow Jesus. This is the universal Christian vocation. However, religious want to make this vocation the central axis of their lives and the primary inspiration of all that they are and do. We have publicly accepted this commitment before the ecclesial faith community and before God. Our evangelical identity will distinguish us. We prove our sanctification when we translate this gift and vocation into everyday life. We define our identity by walking steadfastly toward this goal. Every human being is called also to sanctification, each in his or her own characteristic way. *Religious men and women are characterized by public and ecclesial commitment that they undertake in community to make their lives radically conform to the gospel— in other words, consistently to seek holiness.* Specific aspects of religious life—such as the three vows, the rules of community life, our readiness to serve, spiritual exercises, and so forth—characterize our vocation alongside others. Still, the common denominator of every religious is the call to evangelical holiness. This disposition has relevant consequences.

Major Consequences for Self-Understanding and Religious Identity

We must understand the challenges and contexts of our foundational charisms so as to interpret, practice, and translate them for today in an evangelical manner. I shall not dwell on this subject, because we have already considered it. Our vocation, mission, community, and formation have a single point of reference—the gospel. We always, however, approach it in new historical situations and in response to new challenges. Because of this, our responses can transform what we are in the light of what we want to be by the grace of God: followers of Jesus Christ in building the Kingdom, in the service of the people of God.

Another major consequence for our identity is the need for Jesus Christ to be the center of our lives. This affirmation is so ancient that it would not seem to be necessary to repeat it. Nonetheless, by its very nature the premise does need to be constantly reaffirmed, as is the case particularly in our time. We are aware of recent tendencies to void the uniqueness of Jesus Christ and the universal salvific implications of his person and life in order to further interreligious dialogue. We must, of course, recognize that our understanding, interpretation, and experience of Jesus Christ are also conditioned by our culture, prejudices, and priorities, as well as by how we interpret reality out of our own context. Nonetheless, these various perspectives, however limited, should not relativize an immutable fact. On the contrary, we are intrinsically involved in an endless discovery of new dimensions of inexhaustible truth. If we want our witness and announcement to be credible, we must fully assimilate this christological foundation. The place that Jesus has as the foundation of our lives is the very source of our integrity—matching what we say with what we do.

I see three major dynamics following from our personal and community relationship to Jesus Christ. First, Jesus reveals the Father to us. He lives with the Father in the unity of the Holy Spirit. And we have been given the incarnate Word, who entered our history in Jesus Christ, and the unity and fellowship of the Trinity, by adoption through Jesus. This truth must always be a breath of constant renewal in our lives. The trinitarian foundation is, in fact, the most radical basis for our lives. The identity of the religious vocation in today's world does not depend primarily upon our restoring spiritual practices, and devotional or liturgical procedures. Neither does it hinge upon our capacity to articulate safe theological precepts, nor on our ability to manage our affairs well. Our identity is nourished in the presence of a mystery, which we experience as a relationship of love and grace. It fills us, it nourishes our lives, and extends to everything that we are, as individual persons and as apostolic communities.

This fact is both anthropological and theological. It is not a matter of volition and methodology, of personal effort or group planning. It is, yes, a gift that is offered to us, that we must effectively share with many people, endlessly and forever. On our part it is, also, a free and conscious response to this gift. The primordial evidence of our identity is that we are bearers of this LIFE who is Christ, and which he gives abundantly. It is fundamental that those who are searching with sincere hearts shall find God somehow in us. To evangelize is not to transmit or impose upon someone a set of convictions and procedures. It is to offer to others that living gift that we have received in order to share it with others. It is this gift that will produce fruit.

A second dynamic of this relationship with Jesus Christ is the realization that through the incarnation and life and by the death and resurrection of Jesus, God assures of salvation and saves us from the destruction of the life that is sin. Only God can do this, rescuing us anew for a communion of life with the Trinity and with each other. We have, because of this, confident assurance of reconciliation. We have the continuous possibility of creating and demonstrating love. But what makes it possible for us to translate the divine pardon into fact is our own capacity to forgive, as well. Through the mercy of God who redeems us, in and through Jesus Christ, we find the following evidence of our religious identity. We are artisans of reconciliation, tirelessly willing to be builders of peace—a peace that surpasses all misunderstandings, respects differences, and resolves conflicts creatively and reasonably.

The third dynamic of the relationship with Jesus follows from the way in which, through his life and message, Jesus underscores the human role in distorting, perverting, or destroying life. It is we, men and women of every age and of our time, who are responsible for injustice and oppression, violence and poverty, marginalization and non-communication. We are the creators of the sinful structures that affect our sisters and brothers both close at hand and far away. The liberating Christ rescues and reprocesses a broken and convulsed world and wants us to be liberators with him. He wants to associate us with an activity that is neither a static and individual conversion nor simply an internal spiritual renewal. It is all of this and much more. But it is more importantly a transforming process, profound and all-encompassing, which Jesus himself calls the Kingdom of God. Jesus invites us to be fellow builders of that Kingdom. This concrete and demanding liberating dimension is a fundamental part of our identity as religious. We are called to demonstrate this dimension in complementary unity with every one of the evangelical vocations and professions, each with its own charism, response, and mission. All of us must participate in our own way in making known this Kingdom which comes to us in, by, and with Jesus. We must all build it by what we are and what we do, in the historical contexts in which each of us lives, together walking toward its eschatological fulfillment.

I take this matter of identity and related problems to be the principal challenge that the religious life is facing today. While it is not the only problem, it is where all the other challenges meet and are defined, from which they find meaning, direction, and solutions. Men and women religious must today be proclaimers of the faith, of the whole person and mystery of Jesus, with all that this implies. This must be lived, personally and together with others, in that faith community which, according to the design of God, is an extension of the presence of Jesus Christ in the world throughout time, the church.

Another major consequence for our self-identity is the ecclesiality of religious life. It means being linked to the church, responsibly open and obedient to her. This is another mark of the identity of religious life. The church is a mystical reality, full of divine meaning, and also a human community. She is historically situated in time and space, in culture, and in concrete societies. The church is both the location and starting point of any approach to building the Kingdom in any context. At the same time, the church and religious life derive from their historicity new modalities and objectives of mission, of both presence and action.

Going beyond the dynamics of communion and participation, of salvation and liberation, which we have previously considered, I wish to underscore three major elements or trends that should motivate us today and provide form and identity to the religious life as a consequence of its ecclesiality. First is *respect and sensitivity to the diversity of cultures.* This is the foundation for the process of inculturated evangelization, which is characterized by giving primacy to the cultures that we want to evangelize. They should be the starting point and reference of any evangelization. Because I have dedicated an entire chapter to the subject, I shall not elaborate on this theme here except to draw attention to it in this comprehensive profile. I am emphasizing its importance to ecclesiality. As we have stated, it signifies the inculturation of the evangelization process and the inculturation of the foundational charism.

This challenge must be confronted in all seriousness and without delay. On the one hand, vocations are increasing in the Third World and diminishing in the First World. This means that such things as the character of mission, style of formation, definition and ordering of priorities, and nature of projects and decisions will be increasingly defined within the transnational institutes, with non-Western cultures as the referent. Meanwhile, every culture today, and in particular Western culture, is being affected by the modern-contemporary cultural paradigm. Therefore, the challenge of inculturating the faith within the structures of the crisis-torn culture of modernity cannot be ignored. It is at this point that the church, and with her the religious orders, are fumbling.

The second major element is the common thread that runs through the charismatic expressions of ecclesially attuned orders—*spirituality.* Spirituality joins the central mystery of Jesus Christ—with its implications for liberation and inculturation—to the religious life. Without rehashing what we have stated in the chapter on this subject, let me merely emphasize some facts that were not dealt with. We are not speaking here of an individualistic spirituality that is overly concerned with personal growth and sustained by expensive methods of recollection (for example, in lavish retreat centers) and a privileged lifestyle. I am concerned about an open spirituality that is sensitive to the needs of others, and therefore centered upon mission. In the spirit of Christ, this kind of spirituality will draw us close to the have-nots and needy. It will keep us in solidarity with the poor and discriminated against, immigrants and marginalized, children and minorities of all kinds. A spirituality of solidarity will always be challenged by the evangelical attitude of the good Samaritan, and of Jesus Christ whom he represents.

Nourished by evangelical values, this kind of spirituality will not allow itself to be trapped in purely human and secular approaches in order to maintain harmony. It will, instead, be guided specifically by the living example of Jesus Christ. He maintained his freedom in the face of all of the manifestations of power in his age—religious, political, cultural, economic, intellectual, and status-conferring. That kind of spirituality has the power to embody everything that a society weary of skepticism and rationalism—fed up with the fragile empirical certainties of modernity—finds attractive in the sacred, in contemplation, and in mystery. In brief, it is a spirituality that can bring together the rational and emotional dimensions within the human person and can integrate individual growth and social engagement. It is historically rooted and confidently oriented outside itself—a spirituality of discernment for decision and contemplation for action.

The third element in the identity of religious is fundamentally important in our fragmented world—*insistence on convincing ethical expressions of faith.* As we have noted, faith must be rooted in history and specifically and ecclesiologically applied to the charism of each religious institute, as well as to the totality of the religious life. Neither our experience of God nor a life of faith nor our involvement in evangelization will be authentically Christian if there are no ethical consequences.

Because Christian faith is historically incarnate, it cannot be dissociated from its absolute axiological-ethical implications. The absence of the ethical dimension explains much of the dichotomy that permits outwardly Christian people to profess the faith and cohabit with iniquity, to live comfortably with the production of injustice, violence, oppression, poverty, corruption, and indifference that characterize and afflict humanity.

From an evangelical perspective, it is of fundamental importance that we transcend the ethics of secular humanism. We must turn instead to the praxis of Jesus to find the life values that alone can help us overcome the seeds of death in order to build the Kingdom in the complex web of modern cities and human society. This must be done at the immediate level of our daily lives, and also at the broad level of political projects of national and worldwide impact.

The religious orders present around the world should not only be attentive to this ethical dimension but also promote it personally and corporately through the institutions and programs to which they relate. Our stress upon personal growth and apostolic and pastoral qualifications should neither hinder nor diminish our sensitivity to the problems of the world. This is the "new Areopagus" that awaits our witness, our personal and collective words and deeds, in a new evangelization of the men and women of our time.

Opportunities for Religious Life

After attempting to establish a profile of the religious life in our time, particularly from the perspective of the survival crisis and the challenge of identity, let us now consider the opportunities. I shall begin by calling attention to some new paradigms that challenge us today.

The Insertion Paradigm

In recent decades in both the First World and the Third World, as we have noted, there is movement toward what is called insertion in Latin America. We have talked about this at various points and from multiple aspects. Its chief characteristic is the implantation of religious communities in less fortunate economic situations. This means primarily a change of environment and of geographical location for religious who move from their various centers to the metropolitan peripheries, and on occasion from urban to rural areas. At the root of this evangelical and prophetic process is the growing and ever more consistent concretion by the church of the preferential option in solidarity with the poor, the common people, the destitute, and needy of all kinds.

This is an option because it presupposes discernment and decision. It involves transforming and restating many aspects of the religious life. Among these, as we have seen, are community and prayer life, personal vows, pastoral ministry, apostolic action, collaboration between the diverse organisms and vocations, awareness of the structural and volitional mechanisms of oppression—injustice and violence—and, not the least, what the poor themselves are doing to rise above these situations.

Insertion is nourished by a change in biblical-theological understanding as the Word of God is read and heard in fruitful interaction with the contexts in which the poor live. At the same time, insertion as a form of option for the poor has become the hermeneutical key to analyzing and interpreting social and cultural contexts. The principal result of such a comprehensive process is, in fact, a paradigm which points to a new way of living religious life. *Unlike previous models, insertion into the life of the poor affects every dimension of religious life and has the potential to transform and enrich our understanding of vocation and*

the way in which we carry out Christian mission. We have found this to
be profoundly evangelical and in accord with the praxis of Jesus. It has
inspired the church and various religious institutes to discover new fo-
cal points for formation and community living, as well as new approaches
to evangelization and of Christian living for those who are not poor but
who are capable of being evangelized from the perspective of the poor.
All of this requires transformation of the assumptions and principles
that guide the present world at every level of idea and action.

The Prophetic Paradigm

The prophetic paradigm is clearly present throughout the entire history of salvation in both testaments. Prophets are inspired and sent by
the Holy Spirit. They remind the people of God's program, which is
also to be their concern. Prophets help the people to rediscover meaning, trust, and hope. Prophets interpret the signs of the times and announce the Kingdom of God.

Because all Christians share in this prophetic ministry through
baptism, it would be disingenuous for religious to claim a monopoly
on prophetism within the church. In fact, every ecclesial vocation
receives and should practice in unique ways the prophetic gift. Nonetheless, a religious life without a prophetic dimension would be un-
intelligible. In the religious life, the public nature of commitment to
a radical evangelical project is a constant reminder to activate the
prophetic gift.

Unfortunately, history reminds us of the lack of continuity between
vocation and concrete practice. The orders have become comfortably
established, compromised by power and prestige, and institutionally
overburdened. This state of affairs has troubled many a consecrated
person and institution. Not infrequently, it has been left to the hierarchy
or to new founders, reformers, and holy persons to redirect religious
life toward a prophetic stance.

Today's reality seems to confirm the fact that the prophetic dimension should be a key paradigm and priority for religious life. We are
living in a moment of prophetic urgency. This conviction pervades and
motivates the membership and all the forms and models of the consecrated life, each in its own way. Some of the evidence that I shall now
catalogue has, in fact, been expressed as prophetic concerns wherever
evangelical institutions have begun to reclaim God's project in search
of clear alternatives to today's dominant lifestyles.

1. I shall repeat once more, now under the prophetic rubric, the importance of insertion as a way of opting for the poor. The option for the
poor and insertion allow us to perceive and denounce as a breach of
justice the great chasm that separates the few people and nations that

have so much from the many that have so little. This is the prophetic dimension of insertion.

2. To be prophetic is to search honestly for a simple and austere lifestyle. It entails renouncing privileges and rejecting institutional power of which the numerous properties of the orders are clear evidence. By reducing our personnel and abandoning or substantially reformulating our major endeavors, we can relativize the scope of this kind of power. At the same time we can add moral weight to our demands for justice when we demonstrate the consistency of our words and deeds with the gospel. In sum, we prove our capacity to work together with others when we give up our privileges, properties, and powers.

3. Thorough appreciation for the role of women and their potential in society and the church is required. We have come to realize today how much women in the church are subordinated to male hegemony. God's work has been shattered by continuing asymmetrical relationships between men and women, particularly at the level of creating, shaping, and guiding religious life and its apostolic activities. Our world offers to the religious orders the opportunity to testify to the value of a healthy feminine perspective. We can show by practical experience the contribution that women are making to enriching and broadening our faith.

4. The growing presence, qualifications, and performance of the laity, as they join hands in service, apostolic ministry, and spiritual presence likewise require appreciation. We are discovering the extent to which we have squandered the wealth of their specific Christian contribution as effective witnesses to the faith in family life, at work, and in society. We realize the value of their training in the faith and of their ethical formation, particularly as we face a pluralistic world, so lacking in principles, values, and trustworthy criteria.

We realize how important it is that the lay contributions to the church not be confined to temples and parishes, as though laity were merely filling in for a diminishing clergy. We also sense that the habitual substitution of the clergy by the women's orders should not hinder the laity's advance to new ministries, which may turn out to be a more adequate and consistent response to the serious shortage of priests.

We see a promising new ecclesial reality where laymen and laywomen are more highly valued. In association with religious institutes, they are developing ties to the same charisms and spirituality. We are also aware of the attainments of the many different kinds of international lay movements. To the degree that they are able to inculturate their messages and to freely open up their processes and methods to building justice in the secular world, they will become even more significant. In this context the insertion of men and women religious can be an important bearing to guide us at the crossroad that laity, religious persons, and prophetic movements face. This should not be a matter of defining the watershed which confines the base ecclesial communities to popular (poor) sectors and international movements to the middle classes. Though the paradigms of these approaches to Christian life are different, they can complement each other in the same way as ecumenism and interreligious dialogue. If it has been possible for people of different Christian denominations to dialogue, why should it be impossible to have a critical and discerning dialogue between people who profess the same Catholic faith within a variety of vocations? Might promoting this dialogue be another mission for religious?

Epilogue

Inculturation and liberation, insertion and prophecy, justice and simplicity, the presence of women and laity—these are prophetic indexes of a religious life which is relevant for both the present and the future. They all must be experienced anthrolpologically together on the basis of a trinitarian, christological, pneumatological, and ecclesial identity. They are expressed in missionary, apostolic, and pastoral praxis.

All of the above represent a new vision of religious life that is already being realized even while we look to a future that is almost upon us. These are current responses that the religious life can give to that part of our world that is particularly open to these concerns. Each and every one of these dimensions points to fundamental elements of the divine plan and can be applied to the various forms of church life today. Each concern adequately reflects a contemporary awareness that is important for our times. They all emerge from within the critical awareness and the aspirations of the best of our societies and cultures, which cry out for urgent alternatives for our current world situation.

In this sense, the religious life is not out of phase, nor is it alienated from the world. On the contrary, in each one of the lines of our profile we discern real opportunities for presence, action, and influence. Our responses must be simultaneously cultural and countercultural as we conceive, build, and transform ourselves and our world. They must be faithful and creative in the light of that Kingdom, which is made always available to us in and through Jesus Christ. But none of this has been promised us in advance; it neither follows automatically from a theoretical and ideal concept of the religious life, nor from our pragmatic adaptation to daily living. The real source is an evangelical and charismatic reinterpretation of the complex reality of the world, of the societies and cultures in which we have been called to express our consecration and mission.

This explains why the chapters of this book were not formulated in programmatic terms and why they have not been reinforced with lengthy biblical citations or quotations from theological works or ecclesiastical documents. As I indicated in the Prologue, I chose instead a methodology that would allow me to examine and analyze our concrete, living realities. This method enables us to discover claims and demands on the religious life that are capable of identifying problems, challenges, and opportunities in this world and within the church that must respond to the world today.

This book commends a high degree of faithfulness to and appreciation for the traditions of the religious life. But it also commends an unavoidable creativity that, I trust, is soundly based. Creative fidelity can help discern a religious life conscious of the past and rooted in it while remaining sensitive to the demands of the present. The major challenge for us today is to transcend merely analytical awareness and to attain an existential and affective fulfillment of the concerns we have been discussing—in our personal lives and in our corporate apostolic action. The power of God which is in us by the gift of the Holy Spirit and our personal response, in solidarity, to God's gift, are the promise and guarantee that our aspirations shall be fulfilled.

I am completing fifty years of consecrated religious life. I have been privy to many transformations, and have contributed, in part, to making some of them happen. With immense gratitude I express to the Lord our God, by the hands of Mary, on this Feast of the Presentation of Jesus, my sincerest prayers that all of us, the men and women religious of today, may find definite *directions* that result from clearly discerning the inevitable *crossroads* of history and of life.

Index